INTRODUCING GENESIS

UNLOCKING THE BIBLE VIDEO SERIES

DAVID PAWSON

ANCHOR RECORDINGS

Copyright © 2019 David Pawson

The right of David Pawson to be identified as author of this Work has been asserted by him in accordance with the Copyright, Designs and Patents Act 1988.

First published in Great Britain in 2019 by
Anchor Recordings Ltd
DPTT, Synegis House, 21 Crockhamwell Road,
Woodley, Reading RG5 3LE

No part of this publication may be reproduced or transmitted in any form or by any means, electronic or mechanical, including photocopy, recording or any information storage and retrieval system, without prior permission in writing from the publisher.

For more of David Pawson's teaching,
including DVDs and CDs, go to
www.davidpawson.com

FOR FREE DOWNLOADS
www.davidpawson.org

For further information, email
info@davidpawsonministry.org

ISBN 978-1-911173-80-9

Printed by Ingram Spark

This booklet is based on a talk. Originating as it does from the spoken word, its style will be found by many readers to be somewhat different from my usual written style. It is hoped that this will not detract from the substance of the biblical teaching found here.

As always, I ask the reader to compare everything I say or write with what is written in the Bible and, if at any point a conflict is found, always to rely upon the clear teaching of scripture.

David Pawson

Contents

Part 1	**The Basic Book**	7
Part 2	**Creator and Creation**	23
Part 3	**Creatures and Evolution**	39
Part 4	**Eden to Babylon**	57
Part 5	**Abraham, Isaac and Jacob**	73
Part 6	**Joseph and Jesus**	89

Appendix

Visual aids used in the video sessions on Genesis *Unlocking the Bible* series arranged by parts   **103**

1

THE BASIC BOOK

The Bible is not one book, but many. The word 'Bible' comes from the plural word *biblia* which means library, and the Bible is not one book but 66 books and together these books form a history book – the history of our universe. But the Bible begins earlier, and it ends later than any other history book because it begins with the very beginning of our universe. It goes right through to the end of our universe and even beyond. But it is history written from God's point of view. Therefore, he selects what is important for him; that makes it quite different from a political history or a physical history of our universe, or a cultural history of our society. God selects very carefully the things that matter to him; the events which affected him most deeply. Therefore again, it is quite different from every other history.

There are two themes in the Bible. Firstly: what has gone wrong with our world? Secondly: how can it be put right? I think everybody agrees our world is not a good place to live in. Something has gone terribly wrong with it and the book of Genesis tells us exactly what. But the rest of the Bible tells us how it is going to be put right – or, rather, how God himself will put it right. Only God could solve a problem the size of our world and he is going to do it by rescuing the human race from itself. For what we need to be rescued from is *ourselves*. The word 'redemption' actually means to be rescued; and we need to be rescued from ourselves. So all 66 books form part of one great drama which I am going to call the 'Drama of Redemption' and the book of Genesis introduces us to the stage, the cast and the plot of this great drama, and without the first few chapters of Genesis, the rest of the Bible would really not make any sense.

The Hebrew title for this book is simply *In the Beginning*. That is because the Hebrew scriptures were in the form of scrolls all rolled up and they would simply give each scroll the name of the first word or phrase in it, so just unwrapping the first bit of the scroll they could identify which book of their scriptures it was. When the Hebrew Old Testament was translated into Greek about 250 years before Jesus was born, they changed the name to 'Genesis', which means 'origin' or 'beginning' and that is a very appropriate title because here we have the origin of our universe – of the sun and the moon and the stars, and of planet earth on which we live. Here we have the origin of plants, birds, fish, animals, humans. Here we have the origin of sex, of marriage and of family life. We have the origin of civilisation, of government, of culture, both arts and sciences. We have here the origin of sin and death and murder and war. We even have here in this book the origin of sacrifice, both animal and human. So, it is a remarkable small book of fifty chapters, yet it covers the origin of all that. It deals with ultimate questions like: Where did our universe come from? Why are we here? And, even more personal: Why does each of us have to die? – something we rebel against, something we don't talk about or think about, something we dress up like a horticultural show to try and disguise the horror of it. But we all have to die. Why? Now these are ultimate questions of life and we need answers to them or else we just drown these questions in busyness and forget them. But they cannot be answered by any human being. The historians can't answer these questions. They can't tell us how it all began because no historian was there either to observe or record how it happened. Scientists can't tell us about the beginning of our universe. They can go back to the beginning, but they can't go beyond that. They can't observe anything beyond that. So they can't tell us how it began and therefore, much more, they cannot tell us *why* it began. Science cannot find a purpose for this universe coming into being. They can tell us some details of how it came about, but certainly not why.

Philosophers can't answer these ultimate questions, they can only guess. It is speculation when philosophers try and tell us, for example, the answer to the question that occupies most of them – the problem of evil. Where did evil come from? Why is there so much evil in the world? Philosophers have strained their brains to try and give us an answer, but it is all guesswork, nobody really knows. There is only one person who could really answer these questions for us and that is God himself. So when you open the book of Genesis you are immediately faced with a question. Are you reading the results of human imagination or divine inspiration? Does the book of Genesis just give us another series of guesses from human speculation about these things? Or does it actually give us the answer from the only person who was there when it all began, and indeed the person responsible for it?

There are other accounts of creation in the world. There is one widely known one called the Babylonian Epic. It is far more complicated and far less credible than what you have in Genesis but it is only one of other sagas which are supposed to tell us how it all began. You should read some of them just to compare them with the sheer simplicity and convincing nature of Genesis chapter 1. But you must decide when you read Genesis – are you reading the product of a human imagination or a divine inspiration?

So, you have got to take a step of faith before you open

the book. But, actually, science is based on steps of faith. I have a science degree and I know that in science you produce a hypothesis, a working theory, and then you test it to see if it fits the facts. That is how science progresses. It is built on such leaps of faith, so you leap in faith into a theory and then you test it with the facts. Therefore I believe that the approach of faith is scientific from that point of view and I say: take a step of faith in Genesis, assume it is *God's* answer to these questions and then see if it fits the facts. And there are two big facts that stare me in the face, which are perfectly explained by the answer in Genesis. Fact number 1: what a wonderful world we live in. Isn't it incredible? The universe is amazing, but this planet is the most interesting thing in the universe. It has more variety in it. It has got life in it. We live in a wonderful world, and the more you watch nature programmes on television the more wonderful it appears to be and the wonders of modern photography are revealing so much to us. The other fact is that it has been ruined by those who live in it.

Now these are two facts we all have to live with and we are becoming more and more conscious of the environment and what we are doing to it. A hundred different species are becoming extinct every day. We are destroying the world we live in. Now these two facts are extraordinary. What a wonderful world we live in; and why are we destroying it? I believe that the facts fit Genesis perfectly and I believe it is a scientific approach.

Now let us look at the place of Genesis in the Bible. It is not just the first book in the Bible, it is the *foundational* book for the whole Bible. Most, if not all, biblical truths are here in the book of Genesis in essence – that is why it has been called the 'seed plot' of the Bible. The seeds of Genesis come to fruition later in the Bible, but they are all there in embryo. This book is in fact the key that unlocks the rest of the Bible. Have you ever wondered what the Bible would be like if it began with Exodus instead of Genesis? Supposing this book was missing. I think as soon as you began to read the Bible without it you would say: well I'm not interested in a bunch of Jewish slaves in Egypt. Why should I study their history and religion? Only if you had a particular academic interest in it would you read any further. But because Genesis is there, you are reading about yourself, about *your* life. You understand what makes you tick and why you can't be a better person and the person you wish to be in your best moments.

Have you ever wondered why life is such a moral struggle? Most people want to be better than they are but fail. Why? Well, Exodus wouldn't help you to understand that; Genesis does, because you are reading about your ancestor, a man called Adam, and when you read about him it is like looking in a mirror and seeing yourself. The Old Testament is built on the book of Genesis – there are many references all the way through the Old Testament to people like Adam, Noah, Abraham, and Jacob who changed his name to Israel. The New Testament builds on Genesis even more. Surprisingly, Genesis is more quoted in the New than in the Old Testament. All the first six chapters are quoted in detail in the New Testament. All the major writers of the New Testament – eight of them – refer to the book of Genesis, and Jesus himself did of course.

For Christians, Jesus' attitude to Genesis settles all questions. Because if we follow Jesus then we trust him, we believe he spoke the truth, and it is interesting that Jesus regarded all the characters of Genesis as real historical figures, not legends. He regarded Noah and the flood as an historical event, and if Jesus did then I do, whatever other difficulties there may be, and we will look at them as we go along. Nevertheless, if Noah was real for Jesus then he is real for me. Not only that, but Jesus claimed to be on personal acquaintance terms with Abraham. And he said: "Before Abraham was born, I Am and he was glad to meet me." Jews listened to Jesus saying this and said, "You are not fifty years old and you claim to know Abraham." But Jesus is saying: I was there.

Do you trust Jesus? Then that is the truth. So Jesus was constantly endorsing the book of Genesis. When he was asked about divorce and remarriage, what did he do? He took them right back to Genesis chapter 2 and said you will find the answer right there. So you can see that the book of Genesis really underlies the whole Bible – provides the key to the rest. Without it, the rest would not make sense.

To give you just one example, you will not understand the cross without the book of Genesis, because Paul says this is what happened at the Cross: just as one man's disobedience brought death to the human race, one man's obedience brings life. Now that is the heart of the cross but he is talking about Genesis chapter 3.

I think I have established my case. Therefore, if you don't believe the book of Genesis you can't rely on the rest of the Bible. If Genesis is proved mistaken, then the rest of the Bible is shaken. If Genesis is not true, then chance is our creator. And the brute beasts are our ancestors if Genesis is not true. And, therefore, it is not surprising that this book has been more under attack than any other book in the entire Bible. There are two prongs to the attack. One is scientific and we are all aware of some of the problems there. I am not going to deal with them all in full here, but we will refer to them and there are audio and video recordings and books that deal with them more fully. But we have to be aware of them – especially young people are aware of what they have been told in school in biology classes, they come with that background to read Genesis and they have real problems. We must be honest about them. For example, science has questioned the order of creation, the speed of creation and the method of creation. Science has questioned the age of the earth, the origin of man, the extent of the flood, the age of people who lived before the flood and many other things. But behind that attack, I believe there is a satanic attack. The devil hates two books in the Bible: Genesis and Revelation. He hates the first chapters of Genesis and the last chapters of Revelation particularly, because the one describes his entrance into our world and the other describes his undignified exit from our world, so he likes to keep people out of the early chapters of Genesis and the later chapters of Revelation. He wants to persuade you that Genesis is myth and Revelation is mystery, so that you leave them alone. Because he knows perfectly well that if you can destroy people's faith in Genesis then you have, in fact, destroyed the foundation of the whole Bible. So it is not surprising that there has been such a lot of argument about Genesis. If you distrust this book, you tend to discard the rest.

Now how did Genesis come to be written? It is one of five books which form a unit, not so much in *our* Bible but in Jewish scripture, most certainly. These five books form together the Pentateuch. 'Penta' means five. There is a big five-sided building in Washington DC called the Pentagon and it is the same word – Pentateuch; the five books. They are often called by Jews the Torah, which means 'instruction', and they believe that these five books together form the Maker's instructions. And it is very wise – since the Maker gave us these instructions to get the most out of life – to become familiar with them. So the Jews read through the first five books of the Bible every year, on a lectionary. Every week they read a bit more, so they get round it in a year like painting the Forth Bridge – when they get to the other end of it they start again at the beginning – and it is their weekly lectionary.

Jews, Christians and even pagan historians believe that Moses wrote these five books, and that has been the long tradition. I see no reason to doubt it. By the time of Moses, the alphabet had replaced the picture language that prevailed in Egypt, and still in China and Japan today. But that had been replaced by an alphabet, and remember that Moses was university educated. If ever you see Cleopatra's Needle on the Thames Embankment, it is one of two columns. The other is in Rome and it stood at the entrance to the Egyptian university and may well be two columns which Moses looked at every morning he went as a student. So he had the education and the knowledge to compile these five books, and I believe that this tradition is right, though none of the books has a name in them as author. There are however, two problems if Moses wrote these five books. The first problem is quite minor, and it is that, at the end of Deuteronomy, Moses' death is carefully recorded. I assume you would agree with me that it is a little unlikely that he wrote that. Joshua probably added a note to that effect at the end of the five books to round off the story. But here is the major problem. The book of Genesis ends some 300 years before Moses was born. He lived during the days covered by Exodus, Leviticus, Numbers and Deuteronomy; those four clearly come from his lifetime. There is no problem with Moses writing those. But Genesis ends 300-400 years before Moses was born, so how could he have got his material for the book of Genesis? One of the things we know about early society is that people who don't write have phenomenal memories. To this day, tribes that have no writing can tell you the history of the tribe; they pass it on around the camp fire at night, from father to son. This oral tradition, as we call it, is very strong in primitive communities, and would be among the Hebrews. Especially when they became slaves in Egypt, they would want their children to know who they were, where they had come from.

Now there are two things that are normally passed down in this memory form. One is genealogies, family trees, to give people their identity, and sure enough, Genesis is full of genealogies. There is one phrase that comes ten times in the book of Genesis: 'these are the generations of...' scattered through the book. If you have read it you must have noticed that phrase. That is exactly the kind of thing that would be passed on from memory to memory. The other thing that gets passed on are sagas, I mean hero stories of great things that your ancestors have done. So tribal memories composed of these two things, generation or genealogies and sagas – the things our ancestors did that were exciting – are told over the camp fire. Most of Genesis is composed of these two things. So it is obviously a collection, a compilation of memories that Moses picked up from the slaves in Egypt and put together.

I am sure you can see how clearly that was done. Except for one passage. There is one part of Genesis he could not possibly have picked up that way – the first chapter. Or rather, since the chapter divisions (as so often in the Bible – God never inspired them) are in quite the wrong place, chapter 1 verse 1 through to chapter 2 verse 3 is a section that Moses could not possibly have got from any human being. That section he must have got from God himself. It is one of those parts of the Bible that must have been directly dictated by God and taken down by man. Most of the Bible did not come that way. We must not think of the writers of the Bible as word processors, as typewriters on which God typed out his word, because God inspired the writers to use their own temperament, memory, insight and outlook to shape his word, but so overruled by the inspiration of his Spirit that what resulted was what he wanted written. So that other parts of the Bible have the stamp of the writer on them. The rest of Genesis has the same stamp on it as Exodus, Leviticus, Numbers and Deuteronomy. You can detect Moses' style and hand in it, but Genesis 1:1 – 2:3 is totally different and has all the marks of God's speech. We shall see in a moment that it is mathematically perfect. When God speaks, his speech is perfect mathematics. You see, the Hebrew language does not have figures. They just had letters and each letter stood for a figure, so Aleph (or A) was 1 and B was 2 and C was 3 and so on. That is a common way of counting, and when you turn the letters of Genesis 1 into figures, it is astonishing. I have been in Jerusalem talking to Rabbis who have actually worked out all the mathematics of every verse and they spend days discussing it because it is mathematically perfect. The very first sentence, "In the beginning God created the heavens and the earth" is a sentence of seven words. That is just one of the figures; we'll be looking at this later. But in many ways, Genesis 1 is a unique piece of literature, and has all the hallmarks of having come directly from God. So I can imagine Moses collecting all the memories of the people, the genealogies and the sagas, putting them together and then God saying, Now *I am* going to write the introduction, so take this down.

Interesting that at the other end of the Bible the same thing happens. The book of Revelation was not composed by John, he was simply shown visions and given words and told: now write this down. Of course, at both ends of the Bible you have got things that man could not possibly think up because they are both beyond the reach of his imagination. So God had to dictate, as it were, the beginning and the end of his word.

Psalm 103 says, "God made known his ways to Moses." I believe in handling Genesis 1 (I almost feel like taking my shoes off) you really are on holy ground, you are listening exactly to God's Word, making known his ways to Moses. I have one proof that Moses wrote Genesis 1 down, and that it was not known before the time of Moses and it is this: there is no trace of the Sabbath until the time of Moses. There is no trace of Adam, Noah, Abraham, Isaac or Jacob taking a day off every week. Indeed, there is no trace of the week. Everything is in months, by the moon, and years by the sun. Now because *we* have Genesis chapter 1 at the beginning of our Bible we assume – quite wrongly – that Adam knew it and that Adam observed the Sabbath and everybody else did after that. No! There is no trace. Adam was given a seven-day week as far as Genesis 2 and 3 go – he looked after the Garden of Eden every day. Had a bit of time with the Lord in the cool of the evening. But every day he was working. He had a seven-day week and Abraham, Isaac and Jacob were herdsmen, and cows don't take a Sabbath. I know that; I used to get up at four every morning to milk 90 cows and I would wish they did take a Sabbath, but they didn't. The Sabbath is unknown in nature. It was through Moses that God revealed that he had made the world in six days and taken a day off on the seventh. It is from then on that the Sabbath becomes a feature of life, and indeed when Moses gave the commandment to remember the Sabbath day, he added the explanation (because God created the world) as if this is new knowledge to them, as if he had just told them. So that is a proof that Genesis 1 was dictated to Moses and was not known before his day. There are one or two other indications of that as well.

So we turn, at last, to the book itself and to this amazing chapter with which it opens. We are going to spend quite a while in the chapter, and I want to spend the rest of this section on the first four words – "In the beginning God". Genesis is full of beginnings: the beginning of everything else – except God! God doesn't begin here and that is a very important point. God is already there when the Bible opens. He was already there when the universe came to be. He has always been there. You see, there has to be an eternal something or an eternal someone who was always there in order to bring our universe into being. Because 'nothing' never turns into 'something' by itself. Am I stretching you a bit? It is a bit of philosophy for you – a bit of homespun philosophy – but nothing ever becomes something by itself. There has to be a cause and that cause is either an eternal something or an eternal someone and the Bible begins by saying it was an eternal Someone and therefore the schoolboy's question 'Who made God?' is nonsense. That is like asking whether you can have a square circle. Or, can you fry ice? It is nonsense because it is asking an incompatible question. God never was made. He made everything else, he was always there. Now you must either say he was always there, an eternal someone, or, like Aristotle, you must say *it* was always there, an eternal something. But that is the choice and you have got to choose one or the other, and the Bible clearly chooses an eternal Someone. It is the fundamental assumption of the Bible that God exists eternally, that he has always been there, that he always will be there and that he is the God who is. His very name is a participle of the verb 'to be' – being. Some years ago, I was praying and I said, Lord, please give me an English word to correspond to the Hebrew Yahweh that would give me the feel of its meaning and excite me, and immediately into my mind came this word: 'Always'. That is very close to God's name, Always, he is always there. He *is* Always. That is the nearest I can get in English to the Hebrew *Yahweh*.

In other words, the Bible never tries to prove the existence of God. It is a waste of time as far as the Bible is concerned; he is there and he has always been there, and you assume that. To try and prove his existence, as I have indicated, is a waste of time. He is just there. He does not have to be explained. What has to be explained is the existence of everything else. Now this is the very opposite of the modern thinking which says everything else was always there, now you have got to prove to me the existence of God. But no, the Bible says God was always there and we have to explain now why anything else is there, and that is how the book of Genesis approaches this huge question. By the time of Moses, of course, everybody knew that God existed. He had rescued them out of Egypt, he had divided the Red Sea, he had drowned the Egyptian army. They *knew* that God was real. When you have been through an experience like that you don't need proofs for the existence of God. But I am afraid modern man does, because he hasn't experienced these things.

When you read Hebrews chapter 11, you read two things about creation. First: "By faith we understand that the universe was formed at God's command so that what is seen was not made out of what was visible." And then, secondly, a little later in the same chapter it says: "Whoever wants to find God must first believe that he exists and that he rewards those who earnestly seek him." In other words, the Bible says assume he is there, assume that he wants you to find him and to know him and to love him and to serve him, and then see what happens, but start by accepting that 'In the beginning God' was already there.

Now the subject of Genesis 1 is not creation but the Creator. That is the first mistake we make. It is not about how our world came to be primarily, it is about *who* made it come to be. And in fact, in just 31 verses, the word 'God' comes 35 times, almost as if it's saying God, God, God, God this is about God! It is not so much the story of creation, it is a picture of a Creator. And when you ask what Genesis chapter 1 tells us about God, you find yourself with a long list, and I have made a list here for you.

First, I find out that God is personal. He has a heart that feels. He has a mind that thinks and can speak his thoughts. He has a will and makes decisions and sticks to them. All this is a personality. God is not an 'it', God is a 'he'. He is a full person with feelings, thoughts and motives like we have. Secondly, God is powerful. When our late daughter was a little girl, I remember reading Genesis 1 to her from a children's Bible and, when I had finished, she just sat there quietly and then said, "No sooner said than done", and that was her summary, a good summary; what power! What power just to say a thing and it happens. What authority! You have got to be pretty high up to do that sort of thing. And the first ten commandments in the Bible are all in Genesis 1. Did you know there were ten commandments there? Count them up. Later he would give ten commandments to us, but the first ten commandments were given to our universe.

Next – he is uncreated; he is already there, he always was there. He *is being*, he *is always*, but how creative he is when you learn that there are six thousand varieties of beetle. What an artist, what imagination – no two blades of grass the same, no two snowflakes the same, no two grains of sand the same. What imagination; how creative. We can produce millions of cars of one model all the same. But he has this creative mind; the imagination gives great variety. There are no two of us the same. Look at us – what variety! He is an orderly God; the symmetry and the mathematics of the universe are such that a Jew could find out that $e = mc^2$ and that this applies to the whole universe. It is mathematically so ordered; we will see more of that later.

He is a singular God because all the verbs are in the singular. "In the beginning God created" – the word 'created' there is singular. But he is also plural because the word 'God' is not in the singular, it is in the plural and it is not just a simple plural. Here would be the three words, Eloha means one God, Eloheim means two, but Elohim means three or more and the word used here is three or more. So, in the first sentence we have in the beginning a Creator God who is three but he must be one. Isn't that astonishing? He's a three-in-one in the very first sentence and it takes the rest of the Bible to explain what that means. But fancy using a triple word for God with singular verbs all the way through Genesis 1. Above all, Genesis 1 says he is a *good* God. Sometimes when I have to choose a subject six months before a meeting, I can never think that far ahead so I just say 'Good God', and I said that covers everything I ever want to say. Twice now posters have appeared with a horrible picture of me on them and then 'Good God' above, and meetings have been packed. But God is good and therefore everything he makes is good because he *is* good. That is the message of Genesis. Be under no mistake about this – evil is not God's creation. He is a loving God and wants to bless those he makes. He is a *living* God who is *active* in this world, *speaking* in this world, *doing things* in this world. He is a *speaking* God who communicates to us and wants to relate. He is a God who is like us (if we are made in his image, he must be like us as well as we must be like him), yet he is a God who is unlike us because the one thing we cannot do is create. We can make things out of something else, but we cannot create things from nothing. We cannot 'speak and there it is'. So he is unlike us.

Finally I want to finish this chapter by pointing out that God is never identified with his creation. There is a distinction between Creator and creation from the beginning of the Bible and we must never get those confused. The New Age is confusing them now. The Creator is separate from his creation. He can take a day off and be quite apart from all that he has made. We must never identify him with what he has made. To worship his creation is idolatry. To worship the Creator is the truth and in the next chapter, we will look at some of the other implications of this amazing first chapter of Genesis.

2

CREATOR AND CREATION

I would like to give you a little bit of a philosophy lesson. Everybody has a philosophy. It is your way of thinking about *things*. The word means simply to love wisdom or to seek the answers to big questions, and all of us have a philosophy. But the trouble is in our modern world there are so many different philosophies being thrown at us through the mass media, and in so many different ways, that we get into confusion. If you accept Genesis 1, then there are a whole lot of modern philosophies that are ruled out by the very first page of the Bible. I have just made a list of some of them. I cringe when I hear a word ending in '–ism' . There are only two '–isms' I am happy with, baptism and evangelism, but apart from that, other isms are usually philosophies of a false kind. For example, if you believe Genesis 1, atheism is out. Atheism believes there is no God. "I'm an atheist, thank God", said someone. Agnosticism is ruled out. Agnosticism says: I don't know whether there's a God or not. Well, Genesis 1 says there is, so you can't believe Genesis 1 and be an agnostic. Animism is the belief in many spirits controlling our world, spirits of rivers, spirits of mountains. There is still a lot of animism in the world – that is ruled out. Polytheism, is the belief that there are many gods. Genesis 1 rules that out. Dualism believes there are two gods, one good and one bad, and the good god is responsible for the good things that happen and the bad god for the bad things. Well that is not the biblical philosophy either. Monotheism believes there is only one God. Judaism believes that God is one person. But Genesis uses the plural word *Elohim*. Deism believes that God is the Creator, but that he cannot now control what he has created. He has made something like a watch, wound it up, and now it runs on its own laws, so miracle becomes impossible. Deism is very common, even in church. Do you believe God can change the weather? If you don't believe that, you are a deist – you may believe that he created the universe but he cannot control it. Theism believes that God not only created the world but is also in control of everything and everyone he has made, and theism is one step toward the biblical philosophy. Existentialism believes experience is God. Our choices, our affirmation of our self – that is a religion. Humanism believes that man is god. Rationalism believes reason is god. Materialism believes that only matter is real. Mysticism believes that only spirit is real. Monism is a rather funny one, but it is very common today: that matter and spirit are essentially one and the same thing. Pantheism believes everything is god, and a modern version of it is called Panentheism: God is *in* everything.

Those are ruled out by Genesis 1. If you want an 'ism' that sums up the Bible philosophy, it is Triunetheism – three in one; Creator and controller of the universe. That is the biblical way of thinking that comes right out in Genesis 1, and it stays right through to the last chapter of Revelation.

Let us move on from these rather intellectual subjects and look at Genesis 1 itself, and the first thing that strikes us is the *style* of the chapter. It is not written in scientific language. Hallelujah for that! Otherwise, even in our scientific age, very few could understand it. Aren't you glad that Genesis chapter 1 was not written in scientific language? Very few of us would understand it. It is written in simplistic language. For example, there are only three kinds of vegetation in Genesis 1:

grass, plants and trees. It is a very simple categorisation of vegetation, isn't it? Everybody knows grass, plants and trees. There are only three kinds of animal mentioned in Genesis 1: domesticated animals, animals that we hunt for food, and wild animals. Now these simple classifications are understood by everybody everywhere. Three different-sized plants, three different kinds of animals, depending on their relationship to us. This is what we mean by simplistic. There are only 76 separate root words in the whole of Genesis 1. That is remarkably few. Furthermore, every one of those words is to be found in every language on earth. So Genesis 1 is the easiest chapter to translate of the whole Bible. It takes a genius to be that simple. You see, God – like every writer – has to ask: who is going to read what I write? You have to angle your writing towards your potential reader and there is such a thing as a fog index for writers which I test my writing on, and you take so many sentences, you count the number of multi-syllable words and how many sentences, you put them in a mathematical formula and then it comes out – and you know exactly who will be able to read what you write. It is a good way of checking. Now God wanted the story of creation to reach everybody in every time and in every place. So he made it utterly simple and the result is that a child can read Genesis 1 and get the message, and it can be translated into any language.

It takes genius to be that simple. Einstein was asked to explain his theory of the relativity of time, and he said, "One minute sitting on a hot stove seems much longer than one hour talking to a pretty girl." Now it takes genius to be that simple, and everybody now understands the theory of the relativity of time. God wanted to be that simple, so he didn't write a scientific account of creation, he wrote a simplistic one. God is the subject, along with the Word and the Spirit – there is a Trinity coming in already, especially when later it says, "Let *us* make man." The verbs are very simple, and I want to point out the difference between 'created' and 'made'. The Hebrew word created, *bara*, means to make something out of nothing, and it only occurs three times in the whole of Genesis 1, for matter, life and man. Only at those three points was God creating something absolutely new. In between, he uses the word 'made', which means to make something out of something else. Now we can make things, we can manufacture things, but we cannot create. And that is a very important point in Genesis 1. There are three points at which God does something totally new out of nothing: matter, life and man. We might say today: matter, DNA and man.

The objects, the days 1 to 7 – again, utterly simple. Each sentence is so simple. It has a subject, a verb and an object. The grammar is so simple and straightforward that, again, anybody can understand it. It is a remarkable production.

The structure of Genesis 1 is beautifully put together. It is so orderly, spread over six days, but the six days are divided into three and three. You may never have noticed this, but clearly there are two lots of three days. At the beginning of it all it says the earth was uninhabitable and uninhabited. It was without form and void, or empty, and God takes three days to form it and three days to inhabit it. In the first three days, he creates an environment, but in the second three days he is creating individual things or creatures that inhabit that environment. So he does it in order: he prepares the environment first and then he puts creatures into the environment and there is an amazing correspondence between the first three days and the last three days. The first three days, he creates a varied environment by contrast – contrast between light from darkness, sky from ocean, and land from sea. He is creating distinctions which makes for variety. Having created that, on the third day he put plants in, but now he creates the inhabitants. Now, the sun and moon in that sense are the inhabitants of light. I will come back to that later. There is a very important point here, but light from darkness was general; now we have specifics – the sun, moon and stars – inhabiting that light and that darkness. The sky from the ocean – fills them with birds and fish, and on the sixth day on the dry land the animals and human beings appear. Had you ever noticed that parallel between the first three days and the second three days? Isn't it a remarkable order? It is beautifully done. God is doing things in such an orderly and precise manner; he is actually bringing order out of chaos, which he loves to do.

Genesis chapter 1 is mathematical. The three figures that keep coming through the account, even in the English, are 3, 7 and 10. Three is what God is, 7 is the perfect number right through scripture, and ten is always a completeness. Now, when you look at the threes, sevens and tens, it is remarkable. At only three points does God actually *create* something. Three times he *calls* something by name, three times he *makes* something, three times he *blesses* something. All the way through, even in English, you will find everything is in threes. The verbs are in threes.

Next sevens. Seven times it says, "And God saw that it was good." Seven times! There are seven days, that is obvious. The first sentence is seven words in the Hebrew, the last three sentences in this account of creation are all sentences of seven words (not in the English, I am afraid, but you will have to take my word for it about the Hebrew). Now in all this, it is in marked contrast to, for example, the Babylonian epic of creation, which is so complicated and so weird that when you compare it with the simplicity of God's Word you will have no doubt which rings true.

Well now, I must plunge I am afraid at this point into the problem. But before I do so, let us just underline this point that Genesis 1 is simplistic. I think I can do it most easily by imagining a children's book describing how a house is built. If you want to write a children's book you would have to give a simplified summary. You would say: first came the bricklayer who laid the bricks, then the carpenter came to put the window frames and door frames in and roof joists on, then the plumber came to put the pipes in, the water and the waste. The electrician came then to put the wires in. Then the plasterer did the walls, the decorator painted them and finally they all went on holiday. So, explaining it simply to children, you would probably explain seven stages. But that is simplistic, and as someone who is involved in designing churches and getting them built, I know that life is not that simple. You have to have what is called a critical path analysis, and you work out when the bricklayer has to come and when the carpenter has to come – and he may have to come twice, and the plumber.... It is a very complicated business getting a building up. But the only people who need to know that are the builders. This is good enough, and this is what you would do if you were telling the story to anybody in any time and place. There is no doubt that Genesis is a simplification and that science can fill out a whole lot more details for us, but God wanted everybody to understand that he did it, that he did it in an orderly way, that he knew what he was doing.

But as soon as you talk like that, then this bogey of science versus scripture comes up and the tension is there. There is a tension in many scientists over anything supernatural, and that is because science can only study the natural world, it cannot study the supernatural. So the supernatural is something science doesn't really have any contact with and finds difficult to think about.

But there are specific questions of science that come up in relation to the Genesis 1 account of creation and I feel I must just mention them. Of course, some of the difficulties that people have are flippant. I have been asked: "Did Adam have a navel?" Profound, isn't it? Or "Can snakes talk?", or "Where did Cain get his wife?" Lord Soper was asked that at Hyde Park Corner once and he just said to his questioner, "Why are you so interested in other people's wives?" There are, in fact, three possible answers, but I am not going to give them to you. One of the latest I read in the national press was "Did Noah take woodworm into the ark?", or technically, two woodworms. One common one I get asked today is, "Why are dinosaurs never mentioned?" – since we have become so fond of them. But these, frankly, are flippant. There are much more serious issues that we have to face. The speed of creation. Geologists tell us it was four and a quarter billion years. Genesis seems to say it was six days. There is a little bit of a gap there to be closed. Similarly, the age of the earth, the order of creation. Actually, the remarkable thing is that science *agrees* with the order of Genesis 1, with one exception, and I think that can be explained. The exception is that sun, moon and stars don't appear until the fourth day after the plants are on earth. But in fact, we now know that the original earth was covered with a thick cloud, a mist. In fact, Genesis 2 says a mist covered the whole earth. Science now knows that is true. So when the first light appeared, then it would just be generally seen as lighter cloud, whereas when the plants came and started turning carbon dioxide into oxygen, that cleared the mist and for the first time the sun, moon and stars appeared in the heavens. Now given that actually the appearance of sun, moon and stars after the plants was due to clearing that thick cloud that surrounded the earth, then science agrees exactly with the order of Genesis 1 – that creatures appeared in the sea before on the land; that man appeared last. There is an astonishing correspondence on that one, so order is not now a major problem, but the origin of animals and humans is – this whole question of evolution versus creation. And there are other things like the age of the people who lived before the flood: Methuselah 969, that is the oldest man, and then the extent of the flood itself.

The tragedy is that to the modern mind, these problems come first in relation to Genesis. That's why I didn't take them earlier than now, because I believe we've got to get the message of Genesis first of all, and then tackle the problems later. If you just discuss the problems in Genesis, you will miss the very important messages that it has to give us. But nevertheless, we must not overlook the disagreements.

I want to begin by saying there are three ways of handling this problem of science versus scripture. It is very important which way you are going to do it. The three ways are to *repudiate*, to *segregate* or to *integrate*. I will tell you straight away I believe the third is the right one. The first is taken by naive Christians who say you have got to choose. You either choose that scripture is right, or that science is right, but you must repudiate one or the other, you can't accept both – and that makes it a very simple choice. The result is that unbelievers choose science and believers choose scripture and both bury their heads in the sand. That is not the answer to this problem, partly because science has been right in so much. Just to say science is wrong is probably the most foolish line to take in our modern world. But it is equally silly to say they are always right. But this way of repudiation is not the answer – to say one is right and the other is wrong, and face people with a choice. It leads to dishonesty. It leads people to feel that they must commit intellectual suicide in order to believe the Bible, and that is a mistake.

The second way is to keep science and scripture as far apart as possible and to say that science is concerned with one kind of truth and scripture with another; that science is concerned with physical truth, material truth, natural truth, whereas scripture is concerned with moral truth and supernatural truth, and therefore they deal with entirely separate issues: that science tells us how and when the world came to be whereas scripture simply tells us who and why, and they are to be kept entirely separate; segregate them as far away as possible, then they can live together. It is a rather strange approach.

To try and put it in its modern dress, science talks about *facts,* whereas scripture is supposed to talk about *values* and therefore we don't look into the Bible for facts, we look into the Bible for values. That is a very common way of talking today, even by preachers in churches. But it is the wrong solution. It fits our Greek thinking and most of us think like Greeks unfortunately, and we keep the physical and the spiritual in two watertight compartments – the sacred and the secular, the temporal and the eternal. That kind of thinking is totally alien to the Hebrew mind which saw God as Creator and Redeemer so that the physical and the spiritual belong together. So, I don't think this is the answer either. It involves treating Genesis as myth. Genesis chapter 3 becomes a fable entitled, 'How the snake lost its legs' and Adam becomes Everyman instead of one man. I am sure you have heard this kind of thing, so that these are fictional stories teaching us *values* – about God and about ourselves, teaching us how to think about God and about ourselves, but we must not press them into historical fact. Now if you start on that track and treat Adam and Eve as myth – as a story with a moral truth in it, but not historical truth – then where do you stop as you read through the Bible? At first, people said Adam and Eve were myths, then they moved on a bit and said Noah was a myth. The flood story has truth in it, but moral truth, not historical. Then they moved on and said Abraham, Isaac and Jacob were myths. Then they moved on and said Moses was a myth. Then they moved on until now there are theologians who treat the resurrection and the virgin birth of Jesus as myth: stories with a truth in them.

That is my problem with this approach – where do you stop? Ultimately there is then no history left in the Bible. There are only values, no facts. Of course, it makes it possible then to put the Bible alongside the Koran and alongside the Vedas and other scriptures, which are *values*. But I believe it has destroyed the Bible. God is the God of history – history is his story and we are reading facts. Furthermore, as I indicated earlier, Jesus accepted Genesis as factual. Therefore, this is not the answer to the problem but it is probably the most common way that Christians have tried to get over it.

Both scripture and science are in fact overlapping circles and they are dealing with some things that are the same, and therefore there are apparent contradictions between them which we must look at. How then are we going to resolve? How can we bring them together? Well, we need to remember two very important basic things. The first is the *transitional* investigations of science, and I mean by this that science changes. It is always in transition and things that were regarded as scientific fact years ago are now no longer regarded as scientific fact. Science changes its views. For example, it used to be believed that the atom was the smallest thing in the universe. Now we know that each atom is a whole universe in itself. It was said until very recently that the x and y chromosomes decided whether a foetus became a male or a female human being. I gather now that has been thrown out of the window and it is something else entirely different. You really have to keep changing your mind to catch up. The whole discovery of DNA has revolutionised our thinking about life, because we now know that the earliest form of life had the most complicated DNA in it and that mathematically DNA is a language. It is not a chance combination; it is a language passing on a message from one generation to another, therefore DNA must have a Person behind it. That is changing a lot of people's thinking.

So science changes. It is in a state of transition.

Geology is changing. I read an article by the science correspondent of *The Times*. He said there are now seven different ways of finding out the age of the earth: Carbon 14, radiogenic helium, magnetic field decay, oceanic nickel, etc., and he gave a list of the dates that these new methods have revealed. And interestingly enough, the shortest is 9000 years and the longest is 175,000 years, not four and a quarter billion; well, who is right? I don't know. I think we wait until the scientists make up their mind on many real issues.

Anthropology is now in a state of disorder. What we thought were prehistoric men, our ancestors, are no longer regarded as our ancestors, but creatures that came and went and disappeared. Biology again has changed. Very few believe in Darwinian evolution today. So that is the first point I want to make – that science does change its opinion, and to tie the Bible to any particular age of science would mean that in the next generation the Bible would be thrown away as well.

The second thing I want to point out is equally important. Traditional interpretations of scripture can also change. The Bible is inspired, but our interpretation of it may not be. I think we need to draw a very clear distinction between the Bible text and how we interpret it. For example, when the Bible talks about the 'four corners of the earth', who interprets that to mean that the earth is a cube or a square? The Bible uses what we call the language of appearance. It talks about the sun rising in the east and setting in the west and running around the sky. Who takes that to mean that the sun is moving around the earth? Well, they used to, but it was a wrong interpretation. It is using simply the language of appearance. We need to think again about our interpretation of the Bible, so that we become a little more flexible. I believe in this way, when science is realised to be transitional and our interpretation of scripture is seen to be traditional, then we will begin to be willing to rethink.

I thought I would illustrate this by looking at the days in Genesis 1, and I have found that there are at least five different ways of interpreting the word 'day' in scripture, and I am going to go through all five and leave you to take your pick.

There is, as I have said, a slight discrepancy between six days and four and a quarter billion years, and we need to close the gap in some way, so how are we going to take the word 'day' in Genesis 1? It is a Hebrew word 'yom', which sometimes means a day of 24 hours; it can also mean an era – as in 'the day of the horse and cart is over.' I don't mean a 24-hour day, I mean the 'day of the horse and cart' is over. But there are five different ways of interpretation. The first is to take the word 'day' literally as an earth day of 24 hours. Your problem then is to find more time somewhere, and you will find that various commentaries find more time in one of three ways. The first is by finding a gap between verse 2 and verse 3, in other words the earth it said *became* without form and void – over a very long period – and the six days are God putting it right again. That is a very common theory; you will find it in the Scofield Bible and you will find it in a number of Bible notes – that in fact the six days were the reconstruction of a world that had gone into chaos over a long period.

A second way of finding more time is to find it all in the Flood. There have been various books, notably connected with the names Whitcombe and Morris, which have said that the geological data that we have all come out of the Flood – not very easy to maintain that. The most intriguing way of finding time is that God created genuine antiques. It begins with the theory how old was Adam when he was made by God? He wasn't a baby, so was he 30 years old when he was made by God? In that case anybody meeting him would have said: "You are 30 years old." They would have been wrong, he would have been only half an hour old. Do you follow the theory, that

God can create genuine antiques and that he can make a tree that looks like 200 years old and has all the rings in it? It is a possible theory. God could do that, but all these are ways of trying to take the 'day' literally and find more time somewhere. You are welcome to take any of those interpretations.

Then there are those who take a 'day' as meaning a geological era. That is a long time, an 'age day'. Well that's quite a common theory. Therefore, we are talking not about six days but about six geological ages.

The third is the mythological, which I have already mentioned, that treats the six days as pure myth. It is only the poetic framework of the story, and the main thing is to get the moral out of the story and forget the framework that is part of the myth. That means it is a fabled day.

One of the most intriguing was by Professor Wiseman of London University. He believed the days were educational, meaning that God revealed his creation in stages to Moses, and on the first day of a week in Moses' life, God said this is what I did, and then the next day he told him a bit more and the next day a bit more and a bit more. So these were schooldays of Moses. There are two forms of that theory; one is that God revealed creation verbally in words. But another intriguing one is that he revealed it visually – as he did the book of Revelation to John – by giving Moses a kind of picture show: and Moses saw the light separate from the darkness, then the screen went black and then Moses saw another picture of the moisture being separated from the seas, and in the next picture he saw plants and then animals and birds, and so on – a kind of picture show which he wrote down. But both of those theories, whether in word or picture, assume that the days belong to Moses' school timetable as it were.

The final interpretation is that these were 'God days' – time is relative to God as well as to us; a thousand days are like a day to God and a day like a thousand years. Therefore,

God was saying, 'To me, the whole of creation was all in a week's work. That is what it was to *me*.' And the point of saying that would be that if you take geological time, human life loses all significance. For example, go back to Cleopatra's Needle. If you let Cleopatra's Needle represent the age of our planet and put a 10p piece flat on top of the needle, that's the age of the human race, and if you put a postage stamp on top of that, its thickness represents civilised man. Do you realise we lose all significance in that. Who are *we*? And God, I believe, wanted us to think of creation as a week's work because he wanted to get down to the important bit – that is *us* on planet earth.

Well, that is the theory. Note the length of the seventh day because that has lasted centuries. It lasted all the way through the Old Testament. God's seventh day rest lasted until Easter Sunday when he raised his Son from the dead. All through the Old Testament, there is nothing new created. God had finished creation. The word 'new' hardly occurs in the Old Testament. I can think of once: there is a verse in Ecclesiastes – 'Behold there is nothing new under the sun.' So God rested all through the Old Testament – that was a pretty long day!

Well, there are five different ways. I think you have probably guessed which I am going for, but I am not going to press that – these are interpretations. God clearly wanted us to think of his work as a week's work. That is the message. I am content with that message. I personally believe we are talking about 'God days'. He is giving us *his* angle on it. That was just a week's work to him. To him it has only been a couple of days since Jesus died. Time is real to God, but it is *relative* to God as well and we need to remember that.

Well I have taken just one example there. I am leaving the big question of evolution until the next chapter because that is a big matter, especially if man is included in it. What I have tried to do here is to show you that we interpreters of the Bible need to be a little more flexible sometimes and say we may not have understood it right. And I believe scientists need to be a bit more humble – but many of them *are* becoming more humble as they discover the *random principle* in nature, that everything is not neatly tied up in laws of cause and effect. Science is becoming much more flexible. There was an article in my morning newspaper entitled 'Is Science about to Prove the Existence of God?' – an amazing title to read. A hundred years ago, you would have read 'disprove', but there has been a swing round to a universe that is more open to personal intervention and control by God than it was before. So science and scripture in our day are beginning to move together again. That is all for the good.

I believe the third way that I showed you of reconciling science and scripture – to *integrate* them – is necessary because both scientists and scripture are concerned with truth. We are all committed to the truth and we want to find it out, and I believe science has found out a lot of truth about our universe for us, but it has not been able to tell us the most important truths either about God or about ourselves. For that, we have scripture, and thank God we have.

3

CREATURES AND EVOLUTION

We have got as far as Genesis chapter 2 and there are 48 more to go – so let us look in detail at chapter 2. There is a radical shift in style, in content, and above all in viewpoint. When you read chapter 1 and close your eyes you feel yourself hovering just above the earth, but when you read chapter 2 and close your eyes, you feel you are standing firmly on the ground and looking around instead of looking down. That is because in chapter 2 man has become the centre of the picture. In chapter 1 God is the centre and everything is from his angle and his point of view, but in chapter 2 man is now an individual. In fact, the generic terms of chapter 1 give way to specific names in chapter 2. In chapter 1, the human race is simply male and female. In chapter 2, male and female has become Adam and Eve, two particular individuals. God himself has a name now in chapter 2. In chapter 1, he was simply God, but now in your English Bibles it says he is the Lord God. But when you read the Lord in capital letters in your English Bibles, that means that in the Hebrew his name is there. In the Hebrew, since they don't have vowels, his name is made up of four consonants, JHVH from which the word Jehovah has been coined. But that is a mistake because J is pronounced like a Y and V is pronounced like a W. So, in English pronunciation it would be YHWH, from which we get the word Yahweh. In the New Jerusalem Bible, that word is there just as it is. The Yahweh God – I have already given you the English word 'always' as being very near to that participle of the verb 'to be'. 'Being', 'Always' – that is the name. So God now has a name, man now has a name and later in the chapter woman has a name. There are names here – not just names of persons, but names of places. No longer are we talking about the 'dry land', we are talking about the land of Havilah and the land of Cush and the land of Asshur and the Garden of Eden. And not only has the dry land now got names, but the water has names and there are four rivers mentioned here, two of which we are familiar with today: Tigris and Euphrates. That puts the Garden of Eden somewhere near north-eastern Turkey, or Armenia, somewhere in there actually where Mount Ararat still is and where, incidentally, people are still looking for Noah's ark.

So that locates us, but the significance of the names is greater than that. It is not just making things particular – names make relationships possible. And the big thing that happens in Genesis 2 is that man is seen at the centre of a network of relationships, and the meaning of life for us is in relationship. These relationships, as we are going to see, have three dimensions: the relationship above us, the relationship to those and things below us, and the relationships that we have alongside. So, there is a vertical relationship to the God above, a vertical relationship to nature below and a horizontal relationship with human nature in other people and ourselves.

But before we come to that, let us notice one or two more things. In chapter 1, God is simply described as God – *Elohim*, which means three, and yet three-in-one with singular verbs as we saw, and a God who is like man because man is made like God. That is a very important insight. There is an affinity between human beings and God that is lacking in every other part of God's creation. There is no animal that has this. You never saw a chimpanzee pray. There is something in us that is quite different from every other creature on earth and that something is that we are like the Creator in a unique way. In Genesis 2 there seems to be a change to the difference between God and man – that he is unlike us and we are unlike him and we need to balance these two facts. We are like God, yet not like him. He is like us and yet not like us. And we need to keep that balance in order to have a good relationship with him. The fact that he is like us means that our relationship with him can be intimate, but the fact that he is unlike us will keep the relationship reverent, and this balance between intimacy and reverence is terribly important, especially in our worship. You can become too familiar with God, or too pally with God as if he is just one of the congregation. Or you can become too awed by him and almost shrink into yourself and not be able to call him Father. He is Holy Father in heaven; he is like us and unlike us, we are like him and unlike him and we need to keep that in balance, and the first two chapters help us to do that.

The name 'Adam' means dusty because that signifies what material God used to make the first man, so he is called Dusty and his wife is called Lively, or Eve to you. But they are descriptive names and names in the Bible are invariably descriptive. Even onomatopoeic, meaning that the name sounds like the sound of the thing, like the word cuckoo – that is an onomatopoeic word. In fact, when man named the animals as God told him to, he used descriptions of the animals and that became their names. Names in the Bible are not only descriptive, they carry authority in them. In other words, the person who gives the name has authority over the person who receives the name, so Adam names all the animals, signifying his authority over them, and incidentally he names his wife, which still applies to weddings when a wife takes the husband's name. That has profound implications. So names are important, and with Genesis 2, we are right into names of one sort or another.

Now look at the three dimensions of human relationships. The first is the relationship we have to the other creatures God has made, and the relationship is one of subduing them. God gave us the animals to serve us. That does not mean that we have a licence to be cruel or a licence to obliterate them, making them extinct, but nevertheless it does mean that animals are further down the scale of value than human beings. That is important, especially in these days when there is total confusion. I remember seeing a few women in Australia on a march of protest against the killing of baby seals and I know that those same women would not hesitate to have an abortion. We live in a crazy world where a baby seal is considered of more value than a human being. Jesus was willing to sacrifice two thousand pigs in order to save one man's sanity and restore him to his family. We need to get a sense of proportion. That does not mean we have got to treat animals as if they have no feelings, but it does mean that there is a scale of values and the creatures are put under man to serve man. Later, we shall see, to provide food for man, God cancelled the vegetarianism of creation, after the Flood. You remember reading that, in Genesis 1 and 2, God gave man a vegetarian diet of fruit and seed and made the animals herbivores rather than carnivores. That is a significant thing too.

So, in relation to nature below us, we are to have dominion over nature and rule nature and therefore affect it. We are to cultivate nature and control it. It is interesting that man needs an environment that is both utilitarian and aesthetic, both useful and beautiful, and God did not put man in the wilderness. He planted a garden for him that had aesthetic as well as utilitarian value, much as old cottage gardens in England were a mixture of pansies and potatoes, the beautiful and the useful alongside each other. Man needs more than utility, he needs more than food. He needs beauty around him because he has that within him which appreciates beauty. I never saw a dog gazing at a sunset and saying, 'Isn't that marvellous?' There is that within us like God which needs more than mere existence. We need to appreciate and enjoy things and not just survive.

Well now, the second relationship we have is to God above, and those two trees in the garden are very important. One made you live longer, and one made you live shorter. Those two trees are not magical trees, they are what I would call sacramental trees. God can appoint physical channels to communicate spiritual blessings or curses to us. That is why taking bread and wine wrongly in the Lord's supper can lead you to be sick and even die. They are not magical, the bread and wine, but God has appointed those physical channels of his grace and of his judgment, and so I see nothing strange in trees that had such profound spiritual effects. It is the sacramental principle again. God uses the physical to communicate the spiritual. One tree, the Tree of Life, tells me that Adam and Eve were not by nature immortal but were capable of being immortal. They would not have lived forever by some inherent quality of their own, but by having access to the Tree of Life, they *could* go on living forever. No scientist has yet discovered why we die. They have discovered many ways how we die, but why is it that the clock inside us starts winding down? After all, it is a wonderful machine, the body, and if we keep it supplied with food and fresh air and exercise it can go on replacing itself. I change my skin every few weeks. Most of the dust in your bedroom is your discarded skin, and you can go on replacing broken parts – an amazing machine. Why can't it go on doing that? No scientist can tell us. They are trying to find the elixir of life, the secret of keeping the clock going. But the secret was in the Tree of Life and God was making it possible for human beings to go on living forever, by putting that tree in the garden for him. So man was not inherently immortal, but could be – by feeding on God's constant supply of life.

The other tree, however, was a very significant tree. When you read the word 'knowledge', substitute for that the word 'experience'. For knowledge in the Bible is personal experience. Adam *knew* Eve and she conceived and bore a son. That is what knowledge is in scripture. It is a personal experience of someone or something; to *know*. And God said, I don't want you to *know* good and evil, or to put it simply, I want you to retain your innocence. The tragedy is every one of us has lost our innocence in one way or another because once you do a wrong thing, you can never be the same as you were. You may be forgiven, but you have lost your innocence. It is a terrible thing to lose because happiness belongs to innocence. That is why Paul said: in things evil I would rather be as innocent as a baby. Innocence is happiness, and God wanted Adam and Eve to retain their innocence. So why did he put such a tree within their reach? It was his way of saying: I retain moral authority over you. In other words, you don't decide for yourself what is right and wrong, you trust me to tell you what is right and wrong, and of course every parent hopes their children will do the same. You hope your children won't find out the hard way what is bad for them. You hope they will trust you and keep off what is bad, but that is your parental authority. And God is saying to the human beings he has created: you are not landlords on earth you are the tenants, and I am the landlord and I retain the right to tell you what is good for you and what isn't. The trouble is most of us – in fact all of us in some way or another – won't be told; we are going to try it for ourselves to see whether it is good or bad. The result is you lose your innocence, you can never be the same again. Tragic. Well, that's what the tree stood for. It was saying:

you still relate to me as your moral authority. I still decide what is good and bad for you.

Then the relationship *alongside* – man not only needs to relate to that which is beneath him, and he who is above him, he needs someone alongside him. We need horizontal relationships. There is something rather sad about an old age pensioner who only relates to a cat. There is something not fully human there. Nor are we fully human if we are just relating to God and not to other people. We need this *network*. I love the word *shalom*, I always sign it in books, then my name. Shalom is a beautiful word: it means harmony – harmony with yourself, harmony with God, harmony with other people and harmony with nature. There is nothing better you could wish for somebody than that, is there? Here we have in Genesis 2 a picture of that harmony, and God warns Adam: break that harmony and you have to die. Not necessarily immediately, but the clock will begin to wind down. The reason why God said that is very simple. It seems a harsh punishment for just a little sin, but God is saying that once you have experienced evil, he has to limit the length of your life on earth, otherwise evil would become eternal. Now you can see the sense of that, can't you? That if God allowed rebellious people to live forever they would ruin his universe forever. So he has put a time limit on those who will not accept his moral authority.

Now man needed this horizontal relationship – a suitable companion – and however much a pet may mean, a dog or a cat or a bird can never replace personal friendship with other human beings. In Genesis 1, male and female are equal in dignity and we shall see later in depravity and in destiny. Let there be no mistake, the first statement about male and female in the Bible: they are both equally in the image of God. But in Genesis 2 their function is different, and we notice four things that are all picked up in the New Testament.

First: woman is made *from* man. She therefore derives her being from him. Secondly, she is made *after* man; therefore, he carries the responsibility of the firstborn. The significance of that will become clear in Genesis 3 where Adam is blamed for the sin, not Eve. He was responsible for her. The third thing that is stated is that she was made *for* him. Adam had a job before he had a wife, and man is made primarily for his work, and woman is made primarily for relationships. That doesn't mean that a man mustn't have relationships or that a woman must not go out to work. It is asking what is the *primary* purpose for which God made male and female, and the fact that man named woman in this chapter, also shows how the partnership is to work – not as a democracy. How can it, when there are only two votes, and each has one? But as a partnership in which one has the responsibility – rather than the right – of leadership and that is how it is meant to work in co-operation. It becomes competition when that leadership becomes domination on the part of the man; that simply leads to defiance in the woman and the harmony is broken.

There are many things said here in Genesis 2 which are terribly relevant. Here they are: sex is good, it is not spelt s-i-n, it is beautiful. In fact, God said it was very good. Sex was created for partnership rather than parenthood. That is a very important point which has bearing on the question of contraception. The pattern for sexual enjoyment is monogamy, but actually that means to be married to one person for the rest of your joint existence. Marriage is made up of two things, leaving and cleaving, which means there is a physical and a social aspect which together make a marriage. Either without the other is not a marriage. Sexual intercourse without social recognition is not marriage, it is fornication. Social recognition without consummation is not a marriage and therefore should be annulled. An important point here is that marriage takes precedence over all other relationships. There would be no jokes about parents-in-law if that had been observed throughout history. A person's partner is their first priority before all other relationships, before even the children – that husband and wife put each other absolutely top priority. The ideal here painted of a couple is with nothing to hide from each other, with no embarrassment and total openness to each other – an amazing picture. It is to this picture that Jesus was to appeal centuries later. There are many more things I could have pointed out.

Well now, here is a human being in this matrix of relationships with a God above, with companion alongside and with nature underneath – to subdue what is below, to submit to who is above, and to look to each other for support alongside. That is the picture and these are the three basic relationships which every human being needs, and needs to get right, and when sin comes in, as we shall see, every one of these relationships is spoilt. The whole network is broken.

This is Genesis 2, looking at man in his context as a creature within creation, and the messages that it brings are very clear and very much needed. However, there are scientific problems and particularly two, which I feel we ought to look at briefly here. One is: where do prehistoric men fit in? In other words, modern man's relationship to prehistoric man. And the other of course, is the much bigger question: is man directly and physically related to the animal world? – the whole question of evolution. It would be much easier to discuss evolution if it was limited to plants and animals. It was the inclusion of man in that theory that provoked the major crisis and indeed raises the major question.

Let us look first then at our relationship to prehistoric men. Since various remains have been found and the claim that human life began in Africa, rather than the Middle East where the Bible puts it, this raises all kinds of questions. We need to look at the relationship of modern man to prehistoric man. What does science say about this, what does scripture say, and can they be reconciled? Let us look first at what the Bible says about the origin of man. Quite clearly, the Bible says man is made of the same original material as the animals. The animals were made from the dust of the earth, we too are made of exactly the same minerals that are found in the crust of the earth. I gather that the minerals in my body are worth about 85 pence; it doesn't help my self-esteem, but I know that all these elements will go back to the earth either quickly in cremation or slowly in burial, but they will go back to where they belong and where they came from. So man and animals are made from the same stuff, and that phrase in Genesis 2 that God breathed into the dust and man became a *living soul* – don't let that word 'soul' mislead you. That exact phrase is used of the animals in Genesis 1. They are called 'living souls' because in Hebrew the word 'soul' simply means a breathing body and so, since animals and men are described as living souls, they are the same kind of beings. We are breathing bodies. That is why when your body is in danger of stopping breathing you send out an SOS (Save Our Souls) instead of a SOB. What you mean is save my breathing body – that is Hebrew talk. Again, Lord Soper in Hyde Park Corner was once asked, "What shape is your soul?" and he replied "Oblong", which is good theology. I am an oblong soul. I shall be buried in an oblong box – that is the shape of my soul and the questioner then asked him, "Then where is the soul in the body?" and he said, "Where the music is in the organ", which again was good theology because you can take an organ or a piano to pieces and you won't find the music, but it is there. It is there when it is made into a living thing by somebody else. Now that is important because that word 'soul' in Genesis 2 has misled many people into thinking that what made man unique is that he has a soul. No, that word soul simply means a breathing body. But I think

I have to say that Genesis 2 speaks very clearly of man as a *special* creation and does seem incompatible with believing that man and the anthropoid apes came from common stock, so there is a direct clash there. And the statement that he is made in the image of God, that he is made direct from dust and not from an animal, and made in the image of God, seems to put him in a very special creation category. And the Hebrew word 'bara' (created) is used three times, as I have pointed out, of matter, life and man as if there is something quite new and unique about man.

Historical understanding of man emphasises the unity of the human race. Paul, speaking in Athens, said God has made us of one blood, and that is true. I know there are different varieties of blood, but everything in history points to the unity of our human race at present. I have studied agricultural archaeology a little and it is interesting that agricultural archaeology puts the origins of growing corn and domesticating animals exactly where the Bible puts the Garden of Eden. The earliest traces we have of agriculture are in north east Turkey, southern Armenia, exactly where the Garden of Eden was. I find that an interesting sidelight. But when we ask what science is saying, many people would have us look at this false antithesis. Has science made false investigations into prehistoric man, or has scripture given us false information? Once again, the repudiation of one or the other is presented to us. For example, Piltdown Man (in Sussex) was a forgery – it was discovered to be the jaw of a pig, and many Christians threw their hats up in the air, shouted "Hallelujah" and said, "There you are, science was wrong." But we have to be honest and consider who discovered that Piltdown was a forgery. It was not Christians who discovered that; science discovered it was a forgery. You can't have it both ways Christians, you can't say science is wrong because Piltdown was a forgery when science discovered it was a forgery. We must be honest about all this, and quite clearly science has discovered remains that look astonishingly like us. Some of the different terms – Neanderthal Man, Peking Man, Java Man, Australian Man and the Lekkes have claimed now to have got back to four million years ago and found human remains in Africa. And now it is almost accepted that human origins are to be found in Africa, rather than in the Middle East.

The dating of this is interesting. Homo Sapiens is said to go back 30,000 years; Neanderthal, 40-150,000; Swanscombe 200,000; Erectus, that's China and Java Man, 300,000; Australian Man, 500,000 and now African Man, two and a half million, three million, four million. What do we say about all this? Well the first thing we need to say very strongly is that nothing has yet been found that is half-ape and half-man. There are prehistoric human remains, but there is nothing half and half as yet. The second thing I want to say is that not all these groups are our ancestors and that too is now acknowledged, so that anthropology is now in a state of flux and these are not ours. The third thing: they don't follow a progressive order. Have you seen pictures of a sort of ape gradually straightening up, and getting a bigger head? I could do the same thing with aeroplanes. If I show a picture of the evolution of supersonic aircraft, it all looks so neat, but that didn't develop into that by itself, and just making a picture of the development doesn't prove a thing. In fact, it does prove that there was an intelligence making those things. Some of the earliest human remains had larger brains than today and walked more upright, and in fact the consensus of opinion now is that none of these groups are ours, not *homo sapiens*. Well, how do we deal with this? There are three possible ways. One is to say that prehistoric man was biblical man and what we are digging up was the same as Adam – made in the image of God. Some have even suggested that Genesis 1 was Palaeolithic hunting man, and Genesis 2 was Neolithic farming man.

Well, that is one possibility. The second is that prehistoric man at some point changed into biblical man, that at some point this animal-like or man-like animal became the image of God, and then there is a discussion as to whether one changed or all of them changed, and that leads to more discussion.

The third possibility is that prehistoric men were not biblical men. They had our physical appearance more or less, they used tools, but there is no trace of religion or of prayer. They were not made in the image of God. Which of those three? I am not going to tell you which I think because my feeling is that anthropology is in such a state of flux that we don't need to answer the question, and even if we could, does it really matter? I am reminded of the two chimpanzees arguing and one said to the other, "Am I my keeper's brother?"

Let us move on to evolution, which is the big issue – not how do we relate to prehistoric man, but how do we relate to the animals? I must give you a few terms to go on with so that we know what we are talking about. Most assume that evolution is Charles Darwin's theory, but it isn't actually. It was Aristotle's and in modern days it was Erasmus Darwin who propounded it. That was Charles' granddad, but Charles picked it up from his atheist grandfather and he made it popular. Now there are certain terms we need to know. The first is *variation*, which is the belief that there have been small gradual changes in form which are passed on to each generation. So, each generation changes slightly and passes on the change. The second, is that from those variations there has been a natural selection, which means the survival of those most suited to their environment. In other words, against the coal pit heaps in north east England the black moth was more suited to camouflage than the white, so the white moth died out and the black moth survived. Now that the coal slag heaps have gone in my part of the country, the north east, the white moths are coming back again, and the black moths are disappearing. Which is more suitable to its environment? There's a natural selection going on so that those that are more adapted to their environment survive. This selection is natural, it happens automatically within nature with no help from outside nature; nature herself selects those species more suitable. But that slow, gradual process has now changed. A Frenchman called Lamarque said that instead of slow gradual changes there were sudden huge changes – mutations he called them. It was more like a staircase than an escalator, and there has been debate about these two things.

There are two more terms then we can look at it. The first – micro-evolution – believes that there has been limited change within certain animal groups, within the horse group or the dog group, and I believe that science has certainly proved micro-evolution. But macro-evolution is the belief that all animals came from the same origin and that all are related, and all go back to the same simple form of life that developed into a more and more complex being. One other word that I want to introduce you to, which to me is crucial, is the word 'struggle'. It means the survival of the fittest and that is a concept that has caused more suffering in the twentieth century, more *human* suffering, than almost any other idea. I want to show you how in a moment.

I am not going to argue the case for or against evolution, except to point out that it is still a theory. It has not been proven and, in fact, the more evidence we get from fossil life, the less it looks like being an adequate theory of how the different forms of life arose. For example, in the fossil evidence most different groups appear simultaneously, quite quickly in the Cambrian period. They don't gradually appear over ages, they appear almost together. Secondly, the complex forms of life and the simple forms of life appear together. There isn't a train from the simple to the complex. Thirdly, there are very few bridge fossils that are half way between one species and another. Next, all life – right from the beginning – is very complicated. It always had DNA in it. Next, mutations, sudden changes, usually deform and cause creatures to die out. Next, inter-breeding usually leads to sterility, and so I could go on. Above all, the statistics do not allow for this to have happened. There isn't enough time, that is why a new theory is that life started on another planet, floated through space and landed here. There really isn't enough time here statistically for all these varieties to have developed.

I want to go on to something quite different: the effect of this theory on human beings. Not only has it fed our pride in thinking we have come so far that we are going to go on up and up and up and on and on and on as an English Prime Minister put it, but I want to show you now what has happened with this word struggle. You will find it in American capitalism. Men like John D Rockefeller said, "Business is the survival of the fittest", and that led to untold suffering. You find it in fascism. Adolf Hitler's book was called *My Struggle*, and he believed in the survival of the fittest, the fittest being the German Aryan race and certainly not the Jewish people. You find it in communism. Karl Marx wrote about the struggle between the bourgeoisie and the proletariat, which must issue in revolution. You find it, this word 'struggle', in the early days of colonialism when people were simply wiped out in the name of progress, and I am bold enough to say that this idea, the survival of the fittest, when applied to human beings has caused more suffering than any other idea. But it has also faced us with two huge choices.

What are we really saying when we look at the issue of creation and evolution? It faces us with a mental choice. If you believe in creation, you believe in a Father God. If you believe in evolution, you tend to go for mother nature, a lady who does not exist. If you believe in creation, you believe that this universe was the result of a personal choice; or (in evolution) an impersonal chance: that there was a designed purpose under creation, but under evolution only a random pattern. With creation, the universe is a supernatural production; in evolution it is a natural process. Under creation, the whole universe is an open situation, open to personal intervention, both by God and man. With evolution we have nature as a closed system that operates itself. With creation we have the concept of Providence, that God cares for his creation and provides for it and looks after it. Here we have simply coincidence; when anything good happens, it is merely a coincidence. On one side we have a faith based on fact, on the other side a faith based on fancy – for it is simply a theory. On the one side, God is free to make something and to make man in his own image; on the other side man is free to make god in whatever image he chooses in his imagination. That is the kind of mental difference of thinking of creation and evolution.

But when we look beyond that, we see that behind it there is a *moral* choice. You see, the question we are trying to answer now is: why is it that people seize on the theory of evolution and hold it almost fanatically? The answer is deep down. It is the only alternative if you want to believe there is no God over us. Under creation, God is Lord, but under evolution man is Lord. Creation – we are under divine authority, but with evolution we are autonomous as humans and can decide things for ourselves. With creation, there are absolute standards of right or wrong. On the other view there are only relative situations. We talk of duty and responsibility, but on the other side, people talk of demands and rights. There, we have an infant dependence, we become as little children and speak of a heavenly Father; but here, man is proud of adult independence, man come of age, no longer needing God. There, man is a fallen creature; here he is rising. There, salvation of the weak; here, survival of the strong. Nietzsche, the philosopher behind Hitler, said he hated Christianity because it kept weak people going, it looked after sick people and dying people, but his philosophy was survival of the strong. One view is that right is might – when you are powerful whatever you do is right. One view leads to a situation of peace, the other to war. It always has done. One view emphasises obedience. The other says: indulge yourself. One says that faith, hope and love are the three main virtues in life; the other that fatalism, helplessness and luck are where we are. One leads to heaven, the other leads to hell. I have drawn this out so that you can see where the theory begins to lead, when you think of man as simply a developed animal. I am not surprised if children have been told for ten years in school "You came from the animals", when they leave school they behave like that.

I have given you a feel of the issue. In the next chapter we will see how man has fallen and the effects that had on his family, on his society, on so many other things.

4

EDEN TO BABYLON

When God finished creating our world, he said that is very good – and that included people. But who would say it is a very good world now? Very few would claim that. Something is out of order. Now what went wrong and when did it go wrong? Genesis 3 gives us an answer to that question. All three relationships between human beings and God, between human beings and nature, between human beings and each other, have all gone sadly wrong. Which one went wrong first? It seems almost as if our world is cursed rather than blessed; we have become alienated. Let us look at three facts of our existence. Fact number 1, birth is painful. Fact number 2, life is hard. Fact number 3, death is certain. Why? Why is birth painful? Why is life hard? Why is death certain? Again, Genesis 3 gives us the answer. Philosophy gives us many different answers; some philosophers say there must be a bad God as well as a good one. More frequently, they say that the good God made a bad job of it and thus they try to find some explanation for the origin of evil. Genesis 3 gives us four vital insights into this problem. Number 1, evil wasn't always in the world. Number 2, it didn't start with human beings. Number 3, it is not something physical but something moral. Some philosophers have said that it is the material part of the universe that is the source of evil; or, in personal terms, it is your body that is the source of temptation. That is not the Bible answer. The fourth insight is that evil doesn't exist on its own – there are only evil people. Evil is an adjective rather than a noun. It is persons who become evil.

Now we are dealing in Genesis 3 with a real event in real history and real geography. We are given the place and the time of it. At the dawn of human history, a gigantic moral catastrophe took place. This is not fable or myth, but we do have here a reptile – more a lizard than a snake because it had legs – and most of the Sunday School pictures I have seen were totally wrong, they just had a snake holding an apple in its mouth or something. This was a lizard, but a talking lizard; can we credit that? Well, there are three possibilities. One is that it was the devil in disguise and he is a master of disguise. Another is that God enabled an animal to talk; another is that the animal was possessed by an evil spirit. Now when Jesus sent the 2000 pigs down the Gadarene cliff, demons had entered the pigs. And it is perfectly possible for Satan to take over an animal and therefore to disguise himself as one of God's own creatures, which would tend to fool Adam and Eve because Satan was putting himself below them as it were – and he was the most subtle creature. He was, in fact, a fallen angel.

There are angels. Evolutionists seem to have problems with angels, as to where they came from, but angels are real, they are more intelligent than we are, stronger than we are. And I have already explained the trees. It is significant that Satan went for Eve because women are, generally speaking, more trusting than men. Men are terribly distrustful creatures. But women are more trusting and therefore more easily misled and confused. But more important, Satan was subverting God's order and treating Eve as if she was the head of the house. I am ashamed, however, of my gender because Adam actually was standing by her side and never opened his mouth once. And we need to say that very strongly. So often on television, when a couple are interviewed after some personal tragedy, the husband just sits there with his mouth shut and makes his wife do all the talking. He should be protecting her, and Adam should have been arguing with Satan because Eve had not heard God's words. Adam heard them, and he should have told Satan he was misquoting the word of God. There are three misquotations of the word of God you can make: one is to add something to them; another is to take something away, and a third is to change what is there. And in fact, if you read carefully, Satan did all three to God's commandment. Satan knows his Bible very well, but he can misquote it as well, and he commits all three errors. I am afraid this is not unknown among preachers. To add to God's word, or to take away from it or to change it in any way is to tamper with something that is changeless.

Well, we are not ignorant of Satan's devices and we know how he got hold of Eve, and it is how he will get hold of us. He does it in three steps. He gets you to doubt with the mind, to desire with the heart and then to disobey with the will; that is *always* his strategy. He gets you to think about something wrong first, usually by misinterpreting God's word, and then he gets you to want it in your heart, to desire it and after he has got your mind thinking about it and your heart wanting it, you are an accident waiting to happen – and when the circumstances are right, you will disobey with your will. That was how he got hold of Eve. And we should have learned from this.

Now we see a very different side to God's character, that has not come out yet: the side of God's character that judges sin. It is the holy side of his character. That has not been touched on in Genesis 1 and 2, but now it comes out clearly. God hates sin and he must deal with it. If he is really a good God, then he cannot let people get away with badness. That is the message of Genesis 3. His punishments are in poetry.

I hope you have a Bible that tells you when God's word is poetry and when it is prose. When in prose, it looks like a newspaper column written from side to side, but when it is poetry, you find lots of space and shorter lines. When God speaks in prose he is communicating his *thoughts* from his mind to your mind, but when he is poetic, he is communicating his *feelings* from his heart to yours. One verse in Genesis 1 is in poetry and one verse in Genesis 2 is in poetry, and both are about sex. Isn't that amazing? The first two love songs – God becomes poetic when he considers male and female in Genesis 1, and Adam becomes poetic when he catches sight of this beautiful naked girl, when he wakes up from the first surgery under anaesthetic. And do you know what Adam actually said? I'll translate the Hebrew properly. He said 'Wow! This is it', he said, 'this is it'. He wasn't so keen a few weeks later when he said, 'it was that woman you gave me'. How we change. But those two little poems in 1 and 2 are God's delight and man's delight in sexuality. But in Genesis 3 the poems reveal quite another emotion in God – anger, frustration, irritation or, in theological terms, the wrath of God. God feels so deeply that Eden has been ruined. It is all spoiled and God knew what it would lead to as well. From chapters 4 to 11, we see the results of chapter 3. Chapter 3 is usually referred to as the Fall, when man fell from that beautiful state. Just imagine it hadn't happened. Just imagine that Adam had not tried to blame Eve, or even God. It was that woman *you* gave me. He is trying to pass the buck. Supposing Adam had responded to God's question – I've done wrong and I confess it – and God had forgiven it on the spot. History might have been terribly different.

You see, when God asked Adam questions – "Where are you?" – God knew perfectly well where Adam was – this is a question at the beginning of a trial. Do you plead innocent or guilty? That is what God is really asking. Eve, where have you got to; what have you been up to? He is wanting confession – because when God gets confession he forgives. That is what he was after, but poor old Adam, hiding in the bushes, said he didn't have any clothes. It is pathetic; and have you ever seen the shape of a fig leaf? Can you imagine trying to hide yourself by sewing those together? it was tragic. But that Fall deserved punishment and it got it and Adam was punished in relation to his *work*, and Eve in relation to the *family*. That is very significant. And the reptile became a snake. I once went into a garage full of huge snakes. It was a man's hobby, which I can't understand. He picked up a gigantic boa constrictor or similar, and said, "I'll show you something," and lifted the scales of the body up about two-thirds of the way back, and underneath the scales was the tiniest leg. He said, did you know every snake has legs? They are not long enough to touch the ground so it has to slither on its belly. I said I never knew that; but guess what I was thinking about when he said it! So God shut Adam and Eve off from life and now in chapters 4–11, the effects are like a stone thrown into a pond. The ripples go on spreading out, covering an increasing part of time and space. They go down through the generations and out, through to nations. Moral pollution contaminates all culture, and progress from now on, all arts and sciences from now on, all social and political life from now on.

Now 4–11 in Genesis cover many centuries, but God picks out those things that most affected him and his purpose. You see, God has feelings, that comes out very strongly now and he can be happy, and he can be sad; he can be angry and he can be grieved. We are going to study his emotions now – his emotional reaction to what is happening down there on earth, and the three events which mattered most to him over the next many centuries were: Cain, and the mass weapons of destruction that came from Cain's line; second, Noah and his ark; and third, Nimrod and his tower. These three events cover a long period of human history, but these were the three things most significant to God and what he was going to do with our fallen human race.

Let us take Cain first. Somebody has pointed out that the sin of the first man caused the second man to kill the third man. This is Adam's own family, and his eldest son kills the middle one, and for the same reason as they killed Jesus centuries later – envy. Envy was responsible for the first murder in history and the worst murder in history. It is a horrible thing, yet if we are honest we have all experienced it in some way or another: envy of someone else. Cain and Abel – Cain means 'gotten' because Eve said I have gotten (acquired) him from the Lord, so he was called gotten. Abel was called breath, or vapour. Was he an asthmatic or was he a sort of weak kind of person? Could be. God favoured the younger child of the two, Cain and Abel. God often favoured the younger as we are going to see later, because he did not want anybody ever to think they had a natural right to his gifts and inheritance. So God usually chose a younger person, but that wasn't why he chose to accept Abel's sacrifice and not Cain's. The reason was that Abel had learned from his parents that the only sacrifice worthy of God, and worthy of sinners to offer, is a blood sacrifice, the result of a life taken in death. You see, when God had covered the sin and shame of his parents, Abel knew that God had killed animals to do so. A naughty streak in me likes pointing out that it was God who made the first fur coat, but it was God who actually killed some animals and clothed Adam and Eve. Blood was shed so that their shame could be covered. That is a principle that begins right there and goes all the way through to Calvary. Abel had learned that, so when Abel came to worship God he brought an animal sacrifice. Cain simply brought fruit and vegetables. He held a little harvest festival and it says God had respect to Abel and his sacrifice, which made Cain mad. And God warned Cain: now be very careful, you are in a very precarious position. Sin is crouching at your door and is just waiting to pounce in and get you. But Cain didn't listen, and you know the rest of the story. He deceived his brother, led him away from the home on a false pretext then murdered him, buried him and then totally disowned him, and said he had nothing to do with it. How one sin leads to another.

There is a pattern emerging here and it is that bad people hate good people and that the ungodly are envious of the godly, and this is going to cause a division that goes all the way through the rest of human history. It's a strange fact. It was Plato who said that if ever a perfectly good man lives on earth he will be crucified. That was said centuries before Jesus came. We live in a fallen world where goodness is hated, where people say, "Well no-one's perfect," and excuse the evil in themselves; and anyone who presents a challenge to their conscience is hated. Jesus told us: the world hated me, it's going to hate you if you live right. That is a fact. That hatred of the good on the part of the evil is a fact of human history. We could say that Abel was the first martyr for righteousness' sake. In fact, that is not just me saying it, Jesus said it. He said the blood of the righteous has been spilled from Abel, right through to Zechariah – and, of course, signifying that he would follow.

Now Cain produced an ungodly line of people and it is very interesting what is attached to that line. Music comes out of that line. Metallurgy comes out of that line, and the first use of forging metal was to make weapons of mass destruction which enabled unlimited revenge and terrorism to begin. The first use of weapons was for terrorist activities from Cain's line. Urbanisation came from Cain's line. It was

Cain's line that began to build the cities. Now what does a city do? It concentrates sinners in one place and therefore it concentrates sin in one place, and cities become more sinful than the countryside because of this concentration. So, you can see that all the things we call human progress are tainted by Cain. The mark of Cain is on them and that is the biblical interpretation of civilisation: that however wonderful our discoveries, however much progress we make, it has always got that taint of killing in it. The tragedy is that I suppose almost every single invention of man has been used for killing and some of them have been used to kill before they have been used for healthy purposes. I think of the splitting of the atom as just one example.

Polygamy came through Cain's line. Up till that point, one man and one woman were married for life, but through Cain's line many wives came in and we know that even Abraham, Jacob and David were polygamists. It all goes back to Cain. But at the same time there was a third brother, a third son of Adam and Eve, Seth. And with him you see another line, a *godly* line, and it says that from the line of Seth men began to call on the name of the God, 'Always'. So you see, there are two lines developing here and they run right through human history and will right to the end, until the day comes when those two lines are separated for ever. But we live in a world in which there is a line of Cain and a line of Seth, and you choose which line you belong to and which kind of life you live.

That was the first major event and God said *he* was Abel's keeper. Cain said, 'Am I my brother's keeper?' And God said: I am, and his blood is crying out to me. Every murder involves God. He is concerned; it is his family. Interesting.

Now the next major event is Noah's ark, the story is so well known, not only from inside the Bible but there are many folklore tales of a universal flood, to be found in many different cultures. There is a racial memory somewhere of this event which has popped up in all kinds of places, but here we have the origin of those tales. It has been questioned whether it is real, and I think it is an open question as to whether the flood was right round the globe, or covering the then known world – that whole Middle Eastern basin, later called Mesopotamia, where the huge plain through which the Tigris and the Euphrates flow is really the scene of all these early stories. Many years ago, an Englishman called Leonard Woolley telegraphed *The Times* in London, 'We have found the Flood!' They had found about 18 feet of silt under the clay and sand of the Mesopotamian basin and he claimed they had found the Flood. Well they had found *a* flood and certainly there has been more than one such devastating flood over that whole area and they have found more remains since. Whether they have found *the* Flood, I think is an open question still. I don't know if you have seen television programmes about the search for Noah's ark itself. There has been study of what looks like the remains of a large boat. Whether it is or not remains to be seen. The interest in the Bible is not so much in the material side of this story as in the moral side. That is the crucial thing. Why did it happen? The answer is appalling. It is because God regretted that he made human beings. I think that is the saddest verse in the Bible. I have heard parents say about children: we wish we had never had them. That is an awful thing, and God says, why did I put human beings on that earth? It was a beautiful place. Why did I go and ruin it by making men? This communicates his heart, his feelings, very much and he resolved to have done with us, to wash them out of his hair. What had happened to cause such a crisis in God's emotions?

Well, we only have part of the story in the book of Genesis. We have got more of it in a book written between the Old and New Testaments in what is known as the Apocrypha, in the book of Enoch. Since that book is quoted in the New Testament as truth by Jude and Peter, we can take it that that book is accurate, though it is not part of the Word of God. But it is a record of history and that book actually tells us that between two and three hundred angels in the area of Mount Hermon, sent to look after God's people, actually fell in love with women, had sex with them, seduced them, and impregnated them so that they produced a horrible hybrid, somewhere between men and angels, not in God's order. That is mentioned in Genesis chapter 6 – the sons of God saw the daughters of men, that they were fair; and it called the hybrid offspring Nephilim, sometimes translated 'giants' in English versions. We don't know what it means; it is just a new-fangled term for a new-fangled sort of creature. It is strange that Hollywood has caught up with this, producing films like *Rosemary's Baby* which imagines Satan impregnating a girl. It is a kind of horrible travesty of the virgin birth, where the Holy Spirit came on Mary. It is a strange and weird story, but it is interesting that that horrible intercourse between angels and men (and incidentally intercourse between humans and animals is just as much an abomination to God, as disgusting to him, it is not what he intended), that horrible combination was the beginning of occultism, because those angels taught those women witchcraft and we can trace occultism back to this horrible event. It says that the immediate effect of this perverted sex was that violence filled the whole earth - because the one thing leads to the other: it's treating people as objects not as persons. And violence, it says, filled the earth, and finally it reached a stage where it says that God saw that every imagination of man's heart was only evil continually. What a statement. *Every*, *only*, *continually*, it could not be more strongly expressed, and these were people made in God's image. Can you imagine how he felt? And he said: that's it; that's enough. But being God, he is very patient, and he gave them full warning. He got hold of that man called Enoch who was the first prophet ever to give a message from God to the human race – and the message was: God is coming to judge and he is going to deal with all ungodliness. Enoch, at the age of 65, had a child, a boy, and God gave him the name for the boy and the boy was to be called 'When he dies it will happen'. What an extraordinary name for a boy! Can you imagine the teacher at school? "What's your name, little boy?"

"When he dies it will happen".

"Have you done your homework, 'When he dies, it will happen'?"

Only, of course 'When he dies it will happen' was not in English, it was in the Semitic language. Do you know what it is in the Semitic? Methuselah; and Enoch knew that when his son died, God would judge the world. That is why Methuselah lived longer than anybody else – because God is very patient. Isn't that amazing? 969 years later, Methuselah died, and the day he died it began to rain. Heavy rain. Floods. And Enoch's great-grandson, Methuselah's grandson, was a boy called Noah and he and his three sons had spent twelve months building a huge covered raft according to God's specifications. You know the story.

There is a photograph taken from a film called *In the Beginning – the Bible* in which Charlton Heston played Noah, and when he played his little pipe and walked to the ark, all the animals followed him. It was the most amazing thing. On the first take, these animals just followed him into the ark and you will see that in the film, if ever you see it.

One of the best ocean-going liners was the SS Canberra. When I was at university, back in 1950, I had a friend, John, and while I studied science he studied marine architecture, or ship design, and that was his job. I learned that it was the first ship in history ever to be modelled on the proportions of Noah's ark because he argued that God, who knew the stresses and strains of ocean waves, would know the perfect proportions of beam to length, so he designed it on that proportion. And it was one of the best ships that has ever been built. I just throw that in because you know, it is worth taking the Bible as true. It might just help you in *your* business.

Well, I have told you what happened before the Flood, except that there was just one family, a preacher and his three boys and three daughters-in-law, and his wife, and they both preached and practised righteousness. They lived it, they spoke it and they were laughed at. What are you building a ship here for? Miles from any sea. The sea is coming to the ship, said Noah. They laughed at him. But eight people got saved out of that Flood. After the Flood, God promised never to do it again as long as the earth remained. He also made a covenant, a sacred promise with the whole human race, that he would not only never again destroy the human race, but he would support the human race by providing enough food, seeing that summer and winter and springtime and harvest came regularly. That is a promise God has made, and God put a rainbow in the sky. The reason was that the two things we need for life on earth are light and water, and when they come together you see the rainbow. That is not a reminder to us of God's promise. God said: that's a reminder to me of my promise to you. A bit like God's wedding ring in the sky, a reminder of his promise to be faithful. He has kept that promise, even though people want him to do it again. Lord when are you going to destroy all the evil people in the world, so we can enjoy it? Have you ever heard people talk like that, as if God should come and destroy everybody else, as if *we* are innocent? We always think that, don't we?

Incidentally, when God made that promise he also demanded something of us, and that was to treat human life as sacred, and therefore to punish murder with execution.

That was one of the things he laid down. He said: I will keep the human race alive; I will send you harvest time every year and, believe it or not, there is *always, every year*, enough food in the world to feed the population. In fact, in the year of the Ethiopian and Sudan famine, there was 13% more corn in the world than we needed. It is not his fault, it is our fault. We are just too selfish. So he has kept his promise, but he said: now you are to regard life as sacred; so sacred that if anyone takes it, his life must be taken. I believe that capital punishment was abolished in this country because we had stopped treating life as sacred. I said the next thing would be abortion, and it was.

Well, God made that covenant with the whole human race. The next incident that affected God deeply was Babel. There was a man called Nimrod who was a mighty hunter, but he hunted people as well as animals. He was a man who went to war, an aggressor, and he had ambitions; ambitions for humanity to build a tower that reached even into God's sphere of heaven, to challenge heaven – to build, it says, a *name* for himself, a reputation. We know roughly what the towers looked like in those days. They were called Ziggurats, great big brick towers. They were not stone – because there is no stone in that part of the world, just clay – but great big towers with staircases going up and up and up. On the top, there were usually signs of astrology. But it was not so much worshipping stars that Nimrod built a tower for, it was more to express his own power and grandeur.

Many very tall buildings have been constructed in modern times and you really wonder about man's pride, impudence and sheer confidence, saying: we can build a taller tower than anybody else. We go on in human pride, building these monuments to ourselves – and sheer godlessness behind them. Well, the tower of Babel offended God very deeply and he said, if I let them go on building for themselves like this, there is no telling where it will end. And that is when God gave the gift of tongues for the first time, and he actually gave them different languages so that they were confused and they couldn't understand each other; and from then on, humanity split.

I am not going to expound all these stories. You read them for yourself, I am just giving you keys to unlock. You can see how the Fall of Adam spread out, affecting so many areas of life, and is still doing so. And still there is human pride. 'We can do all this without God; we are almighty.' We see two things through these chapters. We see, on the one hand, God's justice. He always deals with the situation, he always punishes. He has got to if he is a good God, a just God, a fair God. He punished Adam and Eve, he punished Cain, who became a homeless wonderer, a displaced person, vulnerable, defenceless, afraid of being killed. He punished the generation of Enoch – not Enoch himself, but the generation, and we need to remember that God could at any time wipe out the human race, and one day, at the end of the world, he will. Because Jesus said: as in the days of Noah so it will be in the coming of the Son of Man. Just once more, God's anger will boil over. So we see his justice at Babel as well.

But alongside his justice you see his mercy. That is the amazing thing. Even with Adam and Eve, he made them clothing to hide their shame. Even with Cain, he put a mark on his forehead so that he would not be killed, and above all he had this holy line of Seth running all the way through these chapters. There were these godly people, Noah and his family were among them, and they called on the name of the Lord, and through them God was going to save the world.

So we see the justice and the mercy of God alongside. But there is a conflict between them. How should God react when his people rebel against him? In justice or mercy? That conflict goes all the way through the Old Testament. It is only resolved at the Cross. There is a hymn: 'Beneath the Cross of Jesus, O safe and happy shelter, I fain would take my stand', and there's a line, 'where heaven's justice and heaven's mercy meet'. That's when it was resolved.

I am going to close this part of our study in a rather interesting way. Among the people scattered at Babel were a group who climbed over the mountains to the east and went on over mountain range after mountain range and settled when they met the sea. They became the great nation of China, and the Chinese culture goes right back to that day and they left before the alphabet had replaced the picture language of ancient Egypt, the Cuneiform. All languages were pictorial right up to Babel. The language they took to China, they put down in picture form and here is the amazing thing: in the Chinese language, you can reconstruct the whole story from Genesis 1 to Genesis 11 from the pictures in their language. In fact, missionaries can go to China and say: the first eleven chapters of the Bible are in your language. You took the memory of all those events from Babel, and we have come to tell you the rest of the story. It was someone in China who told me this, their word for 'create' is made up of the pictures for mud, life or motion. and someone walking. Their word for 'devil' is made up of a person, a man or a son, a picture of a garden; their picture for secret – so the devil is a secret person in the garden. Their word for 'tempter' is made up of the word for devil plus two trees and the picture for cover. Their word for 'boat' is made up of container, mouth and eight, so a boat in the Chinese language is a container for eight people. We could go on. You can reconstruct the whole of Genesis 1–11 from the picture language of China, and when they first went they believed only in one God, the maker of heaven and earth. It is only after Confucius and Buddha that they got into idolatry. So the Chinese language is an *independent confirmation from outside the Bible* that these things *happened* and were taken in the memory of people scattered at Babel who settled in China. Isn't that fascinating?

5

ABRAHAM, ISAAC AND JACOB

There is a double thread running right through the Old Testament which requires an explanation. On the one side, the Old Testament claims that the God of the Jews is the God of the whole universe. Now in those days every nation had its own god, whether it was Baal, Isis, Moloch or whoever, so religion was strictly national and therefore all wars were religious – between one god and another – or between one god's people and another god's people. Therefore, Israel's God, called Yahweh, or Being or Always, was considered by other nations to be the national God of Israel; and since every nation had its god that was understandable. But Israel herself claimed that her God was the God above all gods – and that phrase is used in the Old Testament. They went even further and said: our God is the only God who really exists; all the others are figments of human imagination. Then they went even further and said, it is *our* God who not only made but maintains the entire universe. Now such claims were of course offensive in the extreme, and you find these claims made in Isaiah, particularly chapter 40, as well as in the book of Job and in many of the psalms.

Now that is one side of this two-fold thread that goes right through the Old Testament: that the God of the Jews is in fact the God of the whole universe. The other side of that is that the God of the whole universe is the God of the Jews, and they were really claiming that the Creator of everything that is – the most distant stars flung into space – had actually made a very personal and intimate relationship with one little group of people on earth; that the God of the universe had become the God of the Jews. In fact, he had identified himself with one family on earth, with a grandfather, a father and a son; that the God of the entire universe was now calling himself the God of Abraham, Isaac and Jacob. Now can you imagine how other nations reacted to that? It was an astonishing two-fold claim that the God of the Jews is the God of the universe, and the God of the universe is specially the God of the Jews. This is explained in Genesis, and without Genesis you would not have any ground for this remarkable claim. As I have said before, if you only had a Bible that began at Exodus, you would think: this is just about the God of the Jews. But Genesis says: no, it is the God of the whole universe who has become the God of the Jews and is not embarrassed to call himself by just three men who belong to that tiny people. Now remember that Genesis actually covers more time than the whole of the rest of the Bible put together. From Exodus to the last bit of Revelation covers around 1500 years, a millennium and a half, whereas Genesis covers the entire history of the world from the beginning right through to Joseph, which is far longer, so when you read the Bible you realise that time has been terribly compressed in Genesis. It covers many centuries; as compared to the whole rest of the Bible, it is a longer period.

Then when you look into Genesis itself, you find a very strange proportion of space given to the different parts of history. Chapters 1–11 form a quarter of the book, quite a short section, and yet cover a very long period – centuries – and also talk about many people, even many nations. But the second half of Genesis, chapters 12-50 which we are now looking at, is a much longer section. It is three times as big as 1–11, it is three-quarters of the book, yet it only covers a few years, a very short period, and it only covers a few people, in fact one family and only four generations of that family. There is a huge disproportion here if it claims to be the history of our world, and yet it is quite deliberate and that proportion has a message in itself. So there is a kind of slowing down of history in the book of Genesis. There is a zooming in from the whole world and all its people to one family, and that is very deliberate because we are looking at history from God's point of view. And God began by dealing with the whole human race and the whole of history, but then he focused in, he zoomed in on this one family as if they were the most important family who ever lived – and from one point of view they were. They were part of that very special line from Seth, of people who called on the name of the Lord. People who call on his name are in his mind – his eyes – more important than anybody else because they are the people through whom he can fulfil his plans and purposes. So that is why we have this very strange proportion.

You see, the Bible is not God's answer to *our* problems, it is God's answer to God's problem. I wish more people realised this. They present often the gospel as God's answer to our needs: Are you lonely? Are you unhappy? Does your life have no purpose? – Then Jesus can meet your need. You have heard that kind of preaching, but actually the Bible is not about *our* needs at all. It is about God's problem, and God's problem is what do you do with a race that doesn't want to know you or love you or obey you? What is he to do? That is his problem and one solution to that problem is to wipe them out and start again. He tried it, but what I didn't mention in the last study was that when Noah came out of the ark one of the first things that he did was to get drunk and expose himself and from then on, the whole sad, sordid story began all over again. So even with Noah and his family, it didn't work, so God had to think up something else, but he already knew what he was going to do to save the human race from themselves, but rather to solve his problem. If somebody asks me: "Why did God create us human beings?" then I give a very simple answer to that: he had one son already and he enjoyed that son so much he wanted a bigger family. I cannot express it more plainly than that. That is why you and I are here – because God wanted more than one son, he wanted a bigger family and that is what he created us for. But the tragedy is that he finished up saying, I wish we'd never had our children. Now what is he going to do about it? He knew, and with Abraham he began *his* solution to *his* problem: what to do with a rebellious human race. Now he chose to do it through one particular part of the human race, and philosophers call this the 'scandal of particularity'. What a phrase! But I want to explain it, it's important. The Scandal of Particularity is, why should God only deal with the Jews? Why didn't he save the Chinese through the Chinese and the Americans through the Americans, the British through the British? It's an offence to us that he chose to solve his problem through the Jewish people. There are two poets, one of whom is called William Norman Ewer and the other Cecil Brown. They both wrote very short poems. William Norman Ewer, who died in 1976, wrote this poem:

> How odd of God
> To choose the Jews

Brilliant poetry, and certainly one of the most widely quoted poems of all time. So along came Cecil Brown and he decided to write a second verse and his second verse went:

> But not so odd as those who choose
> A Jewish God but spurn the Jews

Those two verses sum up the 'scandal of particularity'. Well, we had three children and when I brought sweets for them,

I could do one of two things: I could either bring one bag of sweets and give that to one of them and say, now share that with your brother and sister, or I could bring three bars of chocolate and give them one each. Now guess which brought peace to the house? It was much easier to give them each some sweets, but we wanted to create a family, and if you are going to do that, then you must give the sweets to one and let them share it with the others. That is God's way. Instead of sending his Son to be an American and a Chinese and an Indian and whatever, he chose the Jews. He sent his Son to be a Jew and he is still a Jew; and he said to the Jews: now you share that with everybody else. That is how he chose to save us, and it is his choice. You can argue with it, but that *was* his choice and that is why he is calling himself the God of Abraham, Isaac and Jacob.

Chapters 12–50 are basically the stories of just four men and yet three of them are classed together and one is quite different. Here we are only going to look at the three, and then later at the fourth generation. He is quite different, God never called himself the God of Joseph. He is the God of Abraham, Isaac and Jacob, just the three generations, and we have got to ask why. As we study the stories of these three men, we are going to notice that there is a kind of counterpoint or contrast between these men and one of their relatives. So, the counterpoint to Abraham is his nephew, Lot; the counterpoint to Isaac is his stepbrother Ishmael; the counterpoint to Jacob is his twin, Esau. You notice that those relations seem to get closer and closer from nephew, to step-brother to twin, and God is again showing there are still two lines running through the human race in very stark contrast to each other. And the stories invite you to line yourself up with one line or the other. Are you a Jacob or an Esau? Are you an Ishmael or an Isaac? Are you an Abraham or a Lot? As you read through these chapters, that is the question you should ask yourself. Who is your kind? Who do you line up with?

So it is basically the story of four men. Now there are objections from those who don't want to believe these chapters – who say they are folk tales that arise; that there may be a nucleus of truth in them, but they are simply legends that have grown up around these men. I don't see why people should object like that. For one thing, the novel as such is a recent form of literature. Novels were totally unknown in Abraham's day. Nobody wrote invented stories. Fiction is just not there. They wrote down what happened, they didn't stretch their imagination, much less engage in a mixture of fact and fiction, like many television dramas.

One of the things that tells me these stories are true is that there are no miracles in them. You would have thought if people were going to invent stories about great men of God they would have attached all kinds of miracles. Have you noticed that there are hardly any miracles in the book of Genesis, though there are dozens in the book of Exodus? Legend is usually stuffed with miraculous or magical things happening. These stories don't have that. Furthermore, nobody has found a single anachronism in these stories. Let me tell you what I mean. If Genesis said that Abraham picked up the telephone and got in touch with Isaac, that is an anachronism and you just know that is false because there were no telephones in those days. So, if you saw a telephone or a fax mentioned in Genesis, immediately you would be suspicious. But, in fact, the cultural details that emerge in these stories archaeology has shown to be totally true to the day in which they lived. So really I believe there is no reason whatever for doubting the truthfulness of these accounts.

The one feature that natural explanation cannot account for is that angels play quite a part here – but they do right through the Bible, especially during the days of Jesus' earthly ministry, and even more in the book of Revelation, so if you have problems with angels, you have got problems with the whole Bible. But apart from that, these stories are terribly ordinary. They are about ordinary men and women who are born, who fall in love, who marry, have children and die. So what is difficult about that? They keep sheep and goats and cattle and grow a few crops, so what is the problem with that? They disagree, they quarrel, they fight, so what's new? They erect tents, they build altars and they worship God. All of these things are totally within the range of normal human experience. So what is different about these stories? The answer is that God talks to them and they talk to him; they hold conversations. The God of the entire universe makes a friend called Abraham. That is a wonderful epitaph. Wouldn't you like that on your gravestone – friend of God? It was God who called him: that is my friend Abraham. Now that is remarkable, isn't it? There is the scandal of particularity. People can't cope with a God who makes personal friends. No, they feel that somehow it is not on, and yet that is the truth of what happens here.

Now the big question is: *why* should God choose to identify himself as the God of Abraham, Isaac and Jacob? Why should he identify himself with them? What is so special about them? That is the question people have been asking ever since: what is so special about the Jews? Why should they be the chosen people and not us? Or that is the implication when they say: "Why should they be the chosen people?" You can almost hear them saying to themselves: and not us, because we're so much more important or gifted or whatever, than them. It's not true. But the answer lies in God's *sovereign choice*. Not arbitrary choice, *sovereign* choice. The one thing that is quite clear is that these three men had no *natural* claim on God. God freely initiated the relationship with them; they couldn't say, 'We claimed that relationship,' and in fact in each of the generations it is striking that the son who would *normally* inherit from the father didn't, because in those days the eldest son inherited the family business and the family wealth. Yet in each generation, God chooses not the eldest, but the younger son. He chooses Isaac, not Ishmael; he chooses Jacob, not Esau. As much as to say, nobody has a *natural* claim on my love, it is just my love that I give to you. So, it was not a question of straight heredity through the eldest son. Neither Isaac nor Jacob was the firstborn, and what they inherited was a free gift every time. So they had no natural claim. More striking is the fact that none of these three men had a *moral* claim on God. Not one of the three could claim to be better than everybody else. In fact, the Bible is an honest book and tells us that all three of them were liars. All three of them! We are not given stained-glass pictures of these three great saints. We are given a picture of very ordinary men like us who had their weaknesses. Both Abraham and Isaac lied through their teeth about their own wives to save their skins. So, what have they got that others haven't – why should God choose them? And Jacob was the worst of the three. There is not one of us who would like to have Jacob as a relative. You would be scared stiff of what was going to happen to your money or anything else. He was a schemer; mind you, he was paid back. I cannot read one particular verse in the Bible without giggling: 'and lo in the morning behold it was Leah'. You know the story, don't you? It is the first morning of his honeymoon and he went 'Ah...' and he has got the ugly sister, because he went to bed in the dark and she was veiled all through the wedding, and he had worked seven years to get the pretty sister and his father-in-law has palmed off the ugly sister. Now if it happened to you, you wouldn't laugh, but if it happened to your best friend, well – the humour in the Bible comes across, doesn't it? But the lesson behind that verse is very profound. 'Whatever a man sows, that shall he also reap.' Here is the man who cheated his own blind, aged father and now somebody is cheating him. He can't complain about that, can he? That is the 'biter' bit.

These are very human men – they have weaknesses, they make mistakes, they do the wrong thing, and some right things too. So why should God say, "I am the God of Abraham, Isaac and Jacob"? Well, we must search these chapters for something more. All of them were bigamous, even polygamous. What did they have, then? The answer is there is one thing that marked out these three men. It is a very simple thing: faith. These men believed in God and God can do wonders when a man believes. God would rather have a believing man than a good man; in fact, he even said to Abraham that his faith went down in God's book as righteousness. It was *reckoned* to him as righteousness. The best thing you can ever do is to believe in God. Jesus was asked what must we do, to do the will of God; what does God want us to do? Jesus was quite clear. He said: "Believe on the one he sent." That's all. Faith is the beginning of a good life. You may do many good deeds, but if you are not a believer in God, where does that leave you? God reckoned Abraham's faith was righteousness, and Isaac shared that faith, and Jacob had that faith too – in different ways, for they were very different people, different personalities, different temperaments. But the one common thing was that they had faith.

Abraham showed it by leaving Ur of the Chaldees. There is a big ziggurat there – a tower reaching to heaven – in that place where Abraham lived. It was a very impressive place, Ur. There were typically fireplaces in houses in Ur in Abraham's day. Would you believe that? They were a highly sophisticated, cultured city – terribly advanced for their age. And God said to a man sitting by a fire like that: I want you to live in a tent for the rest of your life. And the man was

75. Would you leave a fireplace like that, and live in a tent up in the mountains, where it is cold and snows in winter, for the rest of your life, at the age of 75? But if that old man had not done so, you wouldn't be a believer now. That was Abraham. He left an amazing place to live in a tent up in the hills and to look after a few sheep and goats – because God said, I want you to come with me – to a land you have never seen, and you will never see this land again. I want you to leave your family and friends. Abraham actually took his father and other members of his family half-way – he got as far as Haram – and they decided they'd had enough, and they settled there. And that old man Abraham went on with his nephew. But he believed God; and even believed that God could give him a son. Well, considering his wife was 90 at the time, it is no wonder that, when the boy came, they called him 'Joke'. 'Isaac' – Hebrew for 'laugh'. What a joke! Because Sarah, when she heard that she was going to be pregnant at that age, roared with laughter, and God heard that laughter too. But what faith!

Mind you, his faith shook a little. He waited first of all eleven years, and the boy never turned up, and his wife got older. When she suggested that Abraham try and get the boy through one of the young maidservants, he did. And that is how Ishmael was born. But Ishmael was not a child of faith; he was a child of the flesh, and God did not choose him. Now don't ever think that that was unfair to Ishmael, because God blessed Ishmael, and he promised him that he would be the father of many nations and produce twelve princes – and he is the father of the Arab nations today. So God didn't put him down, but he didn't choose him – not for that line of faith, because Ishmael didn't show faith, but he was blessed. Above all, Abraham exercised faith when God said: would you be willing to sacrifice your son, your only son, for me? That was after another sixteen years had passed, and then the boy came – Isaac. Are you willing to sacrifice him for me? It tells us that Abraham was willing to kill Isaac as a sacrifice *because* he believed God would raise him from the dead after he had killed him.

Now considering that God never had done that before, and had never caused a resurrection, that was some faith, but that is why he was prepared to do it. And the reason why he was prepared to believe that God would raise Isaac from the dead was because he had been able to conceive Isaac when he was a very old man: when, as the Bible says, his body was 'as good as dead'. Therefore, he said, if God can make my dead body produce life, he can also raise my son from the dead. What faith! Isaac's faith was shown in that he submitted to be sacrificed when he was in his early thirties. Every picture I have ever seen of Abraham offering Isaac was of a little boy of twelve. Is that the picture you have got in your mind? You will never find a Jew believing that because the Jew knows his Bible and he doesn't divide it into chapters as we do. After the near-sacrifice of Isaac, the very next thing that happens is Sarah's death, at the age of 127, when Isaac is 37. So Isaac was in his early thirties, and he submitted to his father Abraham, an old man, and he did it on a mountain called Moriah, which later became Golgotha, or Calvary. It is an amazing story, isn't it? By the way, Isaac also had faith that God could choose his wife for him, and he accepted the wife of God's choice, Rebekah.

The next thing to notice is that Jacob had faith. Mind you at first, he had faith in himself. He could manipulate the blessing and he did, and by scheming and deception he got the blessing, but at least it showed someone who wanted to be blessed, which is good. But later God had to break that man, and he limped for the rest of his life. After wrestling with God all night, he walked like that for the rest of his life, but from then he really believed God – and he believed that his twelve boys would become twelve tribes. These men, in spite of all their weaknesses, their failures and their mixture of good and bad, shine as men who believed in God. They had faith; and therefore, when you look at the contrast in their relatives, you find people of flesh rather than faith. You find materialists, rather than those with spiritual vision. We find Lot who chose deliberately to go down into the fertile Jordan valley rather than live in the barren hills. Abraham and Lot's families had a bit of a disagreement and Abraham said they had better live separately – that is wisdom sometimes –- and Abraham said: Lot, you can take first pick of this land. Where do you choose to live? I'll go somewhere else. It is amazing that Abraham should say that to Lot. It should have been the other way round. But Lot looked down into the valley where the Jordan river snaked through, where there was a jungle, very fertile, warm tropical climate and the whole place appealed to Lot and he said: I am going down to the valley, it looks good. Abraham said: all right, I'll stay up in the hills. But God is a God of the hills and Lot just went after his eyes.

Not only do you see that in Lot, you see it in Ishmael and you see it in Esau. Esau would rather have a plate of instant soup than a blessing when his father died; and he traded it for it and the Esau syndrome is still around. People want everything now, or next Tuesday at the latest. In fact, in the letter to the Hebrews it tells us not to be like Esau who regretted his bargain and afterwards sought the blessing with tears, but there was no repentance there. So we have these three men of faith contrasted with these relatives of flesh, and that kind of distinction runs through most families today – those who live by faith and those who live by flesh.

Now this contrast is also seen in their wives. Ladies, when you read these chapters, study the wives, they are very interesting. For one thing, Sarah, Rebekah and Rachel had one thing in common: they were all very beautiful. Not glamorous, but beautiful, and glamour fades but beauty increases. A friend of mine, a Methodist minister, had a beauty queen contest in his church. This was 35 years ago and it shocked his congregation, but he made one condition and that is that every entrant had to be at least 60 years of age and he wanted to try and demonstrate that glamour and beauty were two different things. Now it says of the three wives of the patriarchs that they were all beautiful and they had the lasting beauty of inner character and they all submitted to their husbands. We'll go on to something else!

The wives of the others are again a contrast to the wives of the men of faith. There is an unusual shaped mountain at the south end of the Dead Sea called 'Lot's wife'. It is the shape of a woman running away. But even Jesus said remember Lot's wife. She looked back to the comfortable life they were leaving, yet a life that was going to be judged by God. They lived in Sodom, a name that has become infamous in history.

Well that is what we are looking for when we read these chapters. We are looking for faith and flesh, and the contrast between men and their wives, and you begin to understand why God says: I belong to this side of the family and not to this side.

Let us just look at those three men in perhaps a little greater detail. God made a promise to Abraham on which we still rely. God began creation with one man and he began redemption with one man, this man Abraham. And he made a covenant – that is a beautiful word that goes right through even to when we take bread and wine together – for 'this is the blood of the new covenant', but this word covenant is very precious. It is not the word 'contract'. It is not a bargain struck between two parties of equal power and authority. A covenant is entirely made by one party to bless the other, and the other has only two choices – to accept the terms or to reject them – but they cannot change them. God makes covenants and he keeps them, and God swears by them. Have you ever heard God swear? When man swears, he swears by a power greater than himself. Some people say: "By heaven I'll do that." Well God, you see, has nobody higher to swear by, so *he* swears by himself. Where a human being might say 'by God I'll promise to do that', God says: by myself I have sworn.

God tells the truth, the whole truth and nothing but the truth and he made a promise to Abraham. A covenant is virtually a marriage, and the key words are always "I will", and if you read Genesis 12, six times God says "I will". The truth is that the God of the universe married himself to this particular family, and he promised them a place to live in; he gave them a little patch of land where the continents meet. The very centre of the land mass of the world is Jerusalem, and that is where the road from Africa to Asia and the road from Arabia to Europe cross, near a little hill called Armageddon in Hebrew, and it is the cross-roads of the world. He says: that is the place I am going to give you forever. And they hold the title deeds to that place, whatever anybody else says, because God gave the title deeds to them – to Abraham and his descendants for ever.

The second thing God promised was to give them descendants – that there would always be descendants of Abraham on the earth.

The third promise was that he would use *them* to bless – or to curse – every other nation. Now that is the calling of the Jews, to share God with everybody, but that can cut both ways. God said to Abraham: those who curse you will be cursed; those who bless you will be blessed – and it is still the truth, as many have discovered. Now that was his covenant. In return, God expected first, that every male Jew would be circumcised as a sign that they were born into that covenant, and second, that Abraham would obey God and do everything God told him, and that covenant is at the very heart of the Bible. On the basis of that covenant God said, I will be your God and you will be my people. That phrase is repeated all the way through the Bible until the very last page, and there it is again: I will be their God and they will be my people. A lovely phrase. God wants to stick with us, he wants to stay with us and live with us; and, as you know, at the very end of the Bible, God himself moves out of heaven and comes down to earth to live with us on a new earth forever. He wants to live with us, he wants to be family, wants to be our Father: that was the whole purpose behind creating our universe and ourselves.

Jacob, the most colourful of all, the mother's boy – even when he was born, he was holding the heel of his twin brother, Esau, the red-haired brother. Grasping from the very beginning, but God dealt with him. Esau actually went to live in a place we now call Petra. You may have seen those amazing temples carved out of the red sandstone. Esau went to live there and formed the nation of Edom, and the hatred between Ishmael and Isaac is still in the Middle East between Arab and Jew. But the hatred between Esau and Jacob has gone – because the last Edomites were known by the name of Herod, and it was a descendant of Esau that was king of the Jews when Jesus was born, and who killed all the babies in Bethlehem to try and get rid of this descendant of Jacob who was born to be King.

Finally, I would just like to point out that Abraham, Isaac and Jacob all showed their faith in one extraordinary way. Each of them left to his son what he didn't possess. Abraham said: son, Isaac, I'm leaving the whole land around you to you. Isaac said to Jacob: I'm leaving the whole land to you. Jacob said to his 12 boys: the whole land I leave in my will to you. And not one of them possessed any of it except one cave, the family vault in Hebron, the cave of Machpelah.

Isn't that amazing! What faith to write a will leaving a whole land to your offspring when you have never possessed it. But they believed that God had given it to them and that one day that whole land would be theirs.

Finally, when I read Hebrews 11 I read about these men Abraham, Isaac and Jacob, and I read about their faith, and then it says this: all these were still living by faith when they died. They didn't just believe for a day or two. When they died they were still believing because they never saw the promises fulfilled. And listen to what it says now in that same chapter: they were all commended for their faith, yet none of them received what had been promised to them.

God had planned something better for *us*, that only together with *us*, would *they* be made perfect. You see, Abraham, Isaac and Jacob are not dead. I have seen the tombs of their bodies in Hebron, but they are not dead. Jesus said God *is* the God of Abraham, Isaac and Jacob, not *was*. He is not the God of dead people, he is the God of the living, and we are worshipping the God of Abraham, Isaac and Jacob. They are still alive and without us they will not be made perfect, and they are among the great cloud of witnesses that is watching how we run, because their perfection, their fulfilment of God's promises, is dependent on us too. We are all going to come into it together. When Jesus comes back to earth, you will see Abraham, Isaac and Jacob coming back with him and, together with us, made perfect in God's sight – all those weaknesses taken away, and perfectly reflecting the image of God.

6

JOSEPH AND JESUS

I think most people are very familiar with the story of Joseph. If you were brought up in church, you were most certainly taught this in Sunday School. It is a story that appeals to children: the goody wins over the baddies in the end; and the theme was popularised in *Joseph and his Technicolour Dreamcoat*. Actually, that is probably a mistake: It was probably a coat with long sleeves, rather than a multicoloured garment, though the New International Version says it was richly ornamented. Certainly, it was special, but it almost certainly had long sleeves and the reason for that is that one boy was always given the job of foreman over the others, and while the others had to roll up their sleeves or wear short sleeves for work, the foreman had a long sleeved coat. Therefore Joseph was put in charge of his brothers, and yet he was not the eldest, so you can imagine the situation that arose in the family. Anyway, that is beside the point. The important thing is that Joseph is the fourth generation – the great-grandson of Abraham – and yet, again, he is not the eldest. There is a clear pattern here. The natural heir does not get the blessing. God chooses in his grace who gets it. It is usually one of the younger ones. And yet there is a great difference between Joseph and the previous three generations. God never calls himself the God of Joseph; angels never appear to Joseph, though they certainly did to the others. And then his brothers are *not* rejected. His brothers are included in the godly line of Seth, so there isn't the same contrast, though his brothers are not too good to him at the beginning. God never speaks directly to Joseph; maybe you have not noticed that. Now he certainly reveals things in dreams and gives him interpretations of dreams, but he never actually talked to Joseph directly, nor, so far as the record goes, does Joseph ever talk to him. So there is a difference here, and when you read through the book of Genesis you are aware that somehow Joseph stands on his own.

Why? What is so different about him? Why are we told his story? Well one obvious reason is that in the very next book in the Bible we find all this family in Egypt in slavery, and somehow you have got to explain how they got there. Of course, the story of Joseph is the vital link of how Jacob and his family migrated down to Egypt – for the same reason as Abraham and Isaac had once gone down to Egypt, for famine, shortage of food, whereas Egypt doesn't depend on rain. It has the Nile coming down from the Ethiopian highlands, so it has a constant supply of moisture in the Nile whereas the land of Israel depends totally on rain for the crops which the west wind from the Mediterranean brings. So at least the story of Joseph is there to link us with the next part of the Bible. And the curtain falls after Joseph, for some four hundred years, of which we know nothing, and when it lifts again the family has become a people of many hundreds of thousands, but they are slaves in Egypt. Well if that is the only reason that the story of Joseph is there, then it hardly explains why so much space is given to his story. Isaac and Jacob had far less. So what is so important about this man? Why are we told in such detail? Is it simply the example of a good man, and a moral that good triumphs in the end? No, it is much more than that.

There are at least four levels at which you can read the story of Joseph. The first is simply the human level. It is a vivid story told superbly with very real characters. It is a great adventure, stranger than fiction. There are some extraordinary coincidences in it and you could really summarise Joseph's life in two chapters: chapter 1, down; and chapter 2, up. That is what happened to him. He went all the way down from being the favourite son of his father, to becoming a household slave, and he went all the way up from being a forgotten prisoner to being Prime Minister. It is an astonishing story – all the way down the social ladder and all the way up again to the very top. Something about that appeals to us, and in between we have got the envy of his brothers – and the key to it all seems to be dreams. Mind you, I don't think Joseph was the most tactful person in the Bible. I think he was quite tactless. Fancy telling his brothers: I had a dream in which you all bowed down to me. That is not the way to win friends and influence people, but it was the truth. He had the dream, whether he should have shared it or not. But then we all make mistakes about when we should share revelations from God, so we must not blame him for that. That is one level – it's a human story and it made a jolly good musical show in London's West End. I saw it, and many schools have put it on as well.

Now the second level at which you can read the story is to read it from God's angle. God is in this story. Even though he does not actually talk to Joseph, he is behind the scene. He is the invisible God arranging circumstances for *his* purposes and plans, and he chose to reveal through dreams. People will accept things in dreams more easily than when they are awake. I have some very peculiar dreams, usually of arriving at a meeting on the wrong day with the wrong notes at the wrong time and I wake up sweating – it is more a nightmare. But it is funny – in dreams you accept anything as real and sometimes God needs to speak this way to communicate with us, but it always needs an interpretation.

Joseph said these dreams were of God and that the

interpretation would come from God. Daniel would be noted for the same gift. God is in fact the main actor in the story, though that doesn't come out in the musical. God is behind the scenes organising all this – no direct miracles, but providential circumstances, and often that is a way that God works. It is not so spectacular or so sensational, but God has a way of arranging meetings with people, and the course of your life is changed. He is behind the scenes bringing about the fulfilment of his purpose – his overruling.

This is the very opposite of believing in luck. I don't know if you know, but the Hebrew word for luck is 'gad' and you may have heard the phrase 'by gad' in former days. You can either live by God or by gad (horseshoes at weddings and all that kind of thing). It is amazing how many people live by luck – and the national lottery. People believe that circumstances are the result of chance, of luck.

But Joseph didn't believe that. He believed that his circumstances were overruled by God and that God was behind the things that happened to him. He didn't see that at the time, but he saw it later, and you can often see God's hand on your life in hindsight, where you didn't realise at the time what was happening. In fact, the key verse in the story of Joseph is 45:7. He finally made himself known to his brothers after humbling them greatly and embarrassing them. He finally forgave them what they had done to him, selling him into slavery and he said: "But God sent me ahead of you to preserve for you a remnant on the earth and to save your lives by a great deliverance." Now that is a very important statement. *God sent me ahead of you*. They thought they had got rid of their brother and sold him to some travelling camel traders as a slave, and that's that. They had taken that special coat of his and covered it with the blood of a goat and took it back to poor old Jacob and said, we found this in the field; your favourite son must be dead. A terrible thing to do, especially to old Jacob, but – "God sent me ahead of you." You see, God allows things to happen; he doesn't force anyone to do harm to another, but he does allow it and sometimes he allows it for his own purposes; and that was the faith that Joseph had – that "God sent me ahead of you." Of course, that was in fact the result, because he became the minister of food. He had interpreted the dream of Pharaoh that there would be seven fat years with good harvest, and seven lean years to follow, and he had said: We'd better store up food now, and then we'll have enough to live on. His foresight through that dream actually saved the whole nation of Egypt, and his own family when they were short of food and came to Egypt. So he became their saviour.

God actually wanted his people in Egypt and this was how it happened. Why should God want them in Egypt when he had promised them the land of Israel, or the land of Canaan? The answer was actually given to Abraham – years previously. God said to Abraham, I'll have to leave your family in Egypt for four hundred years *until the wickedness of the Amorites is complete*. In other words, God would not let them take the promised land from those living in it until those living in it became so dreadful that they had forfeited their right to their lives, never mind their land. So God is a *moral God*; he would not just push people out and push his own people in. It was only when the inhabitants became so dreadful – and archaeology has revealed how dreadful. Venereal diseases were everywhere in the land of Canaan. They were corrupt, they were decadent, and it was only when they reached the point of no return that God said: *now* you can have their land. So, any complaint about God's injustice in giving that land to the Jews is quite mistaken, but he had to keep them out of the land until the state of the people in that land was so bad that being pushed out of it was just judgment.

But there were other reasons too. God wanted them to become slaves. It was all part of his plan to rescue them from slavery so that they would be so grateful to him, they would then live his way and become a model – for the whole world to see – of how blessed people are when they live under the government of heaven. That was the plan. So he let them get into such problems, working seven days a week – no pay, no land of their own, no money of their own, nothing of their own; and it was then that he reached down and rescued them with his mighty hand. So that you see it all had to happen, and God let it happen, for his own purposes. He wanted to redeem them and rescue them so that they would know it was God who got them out, and into their own land. So that is God's angle on the story.

But we still haven't really got to the heart of the matter. The next approach – or level – at which we could read it would be a study of Joseph's character and this is a very remarkable thing because there is *nothing* said about Joseph that is bad. We have seen already that the Bible tells the whole truth about Abraham, Isaac and Jacob, and they certainly had their weaknesses and sins, but not one word of criticism is levelled at Joseph. I have told you already the worst thing he ever did which was just to be a bit tactless and tell his brothers about the dream, but there is no trace whatever of a wrong attitude or reaction in Joseph's character – even his reactions to going all the way down the social ladder. There is no trace of resentment, no complaining, no saying: why has God done this? No sense of injustice that he should finish up in prison on death row in Pharaoh's jail. Furthermore, even though he was far from home and totally unknown, he maintained his integrity when Potiphar's wife tried to seduce him. And when she tried, his reaction was: how could I sin against God like this – and you know that she falsely accused him then, which put him on death row in the jail, but there was not one word of criticism, even of Potiphar's wife. This is an astonishing portrait. Furthermore, even at rock bottom, his concern seems to have been primarily to help others. There was Pharaoh's cup bearer and his baker on death row and Joseph sought to comfort *them*. He is a man who seems to have no concern for himself, but a deep concern for everybody else, and all the way down he never once questioned God, never once doubted that God knew what he was doing, whereas we do. Then there is his reaction to going up to the top. I don't know which is the bigger test of a man's character – being taken all the way down to the bottom or being lifted up to the top. I think probably the second is the biggest test of his character. But look at his reaction to the brothers who had sold him into slavery. He gave them food and he wouldn't charge them for it, he put the money back in their sacks. He forgave them with tears, he interceded for them with Pharaoh, and he purchased for them the best land in the Nile delta, a land called Goshen, and said: I'm going to look after you. They had thrown him out and told his old dad he was dead, but here he is providing every need of theirs. What a man!

So Joseph is unspoiled, either by humiliation or by honour. He is a man of total integrity. He is the only one so presented in the Old Testament. There isn't any other character presented like this, even King David – you know what his faults were, and you will find in every other full portrait we get the whole picture, but here the whole picture seems to be blameless. Very unusual. We read of David's sin, we read of Elijah's cowardice, we read all the weaknesses and we know that, as the New Testament says of Elijah, they were men of like passions to ourselves. But here is a man who has utter integrity. There is only one person in the Old Testament like this and there is only one person in the New Testament like this, and you know who that is.

Now there is one chapter in the middle of the story of Joseph that comes as a shock. It is about his brother Judah, and if you have read through Genesis recently, you must have felt what a shock it is. Suddenly in the middle of the story of this good man, there is actually a contrast in his own brother Judah, a man who visits a prostitute who is actually his daughter-in-law with a veil on, and incest happens and it is a sordid story. Suddenly that story comes, right in the middle of the Joseph story. It is almost as if to highlight Joseph and to say his brothers were bad people but Joseph wasn't. The contrast is marked; I can only think of that as the reason why that sordid instance of Judah is put right suddenly in the middle with no connection as if, just as Abraham had a contrast with Lot and Isaac with Ishmael and Jacob with Esau, here is a brother who highlights the integrity of this man.

So, we are getting very near to the reason why the story of Joseph is there, but we have not yet got there. I want you to put together in your minds the three levels at which we have discussed this story so far. The human story of a man who was taken down to the bottom and then right up to the top, and who became and is called the saviour of his people and the Lord of Egypt. Then we are looking at God's overruling of this man's life that he allowed that to happen and planned it – to save his people. And then we have looked at a man of total integrity who, all the way down and all the way up, remained a man of truth and honest goodness. Who does that remind you of? The answer is Jesus himself. Joseph becomes what we call a 'type' of Jesus, a foreshadowing of Jesus, way back in the Old Testament. It is as if God is showing us in the life of Joseph what he was going to do with his own Son. Jesus, God's only begotten Son, our Saviour and Lord, would be rejected by his brethren (as Joseph had been rejected), was taken all the way down to utter humiliation, and was then raised – in the case of Jesus, of course, raised from the dead. The parallels are remarkable. The more you read the story of Joseph the more you see this picture of Jesus – as if God all along knew what he was going to do and was going to give hints to his people. We find that right the way through the Old Testament. One of my favourite little books is *Christ in all the Scriptures* by Mrs A.M. Hodgkin. She goes through every one of the 66 books in the Bible and shows us Jesus in that book. You see, Jesus himself said, "Search the scriptures for they bear witness of *me*" and yet he is talking about the *Old* Testament. Now when you read the Old Testament, you should be looking for Jesus – for his likeness, for his shadow. Jesus is himself the substance, but his shadow falls right across the pages of the Old Testament, and especially in Genesis.

Abraham, Isaac and Jacob are models of our faith in God, and Joseph is a model of God's response to that faith and how he can take the life of a man and deliver his people from their need and lift him up to be saviour and lord. Once you have got that key, you start turning back the pages of Genesis and suddenly you find Jesus in so many different places, and I want to take you through five of them. There are others that you can look for. The first: all the genealogies of Genesis are in fact the genealogy of our Lord Jesus Christ; and if you read Matthew 1 and Luke 3, you will see those genealogies; you will find in Luke 3:24 names from the book of Genesis. He is in this line of Seth; that line comes straight down to the son of Mary. So, we are reading his life line and if you are in Christ you are reading your own family tree. This is *our* genealogy, these are the most important ancestors *we* have – because through faith in Christ you become a son of Abraham, you have become part of this line. You are in Christ and you have inherited this history, so you are not reading about *their* history now, you are reading about *our* history now. This is your family tree. My wife and I went to Petworth House for a day out, and that was owned by the

Dukes of Northumberland, the Percys, and coming from Northumberland I was very interested. I went to college with one of the Percys and so I was interested when I saw their family tree on a long chart on the wall – and they had traced it right back to Adam! I felt like saying I could do that if only I knew some of the names in the gaps. We all go back to Adam, but we all go back to Abraham. In Christ, this is our genealogy because it was his; it is Jesus' family tree that you are reading in Genesis.

The next thing I want to say is that again and again you look at someone in Genesis and you see Jesus. You look at Joseph and you see Jesus; you look at Isaac and you see Jesus. Let us go back to the time when Abraham was told to offer Isaac. He was told to go to a specific mountain. Years later, that mountain was Mount Moriah, Mount Golgotha, Mount Calvary – the place where God sacrificed his only begotten Son. It is interesting that in Genesis 24, it says Isaac was Abraham's only beloved son and I have told you already that Isaac was not a boy, he was in his early thirties when that happened, and therefore he was strong enough to resist his father, but he submitted to being bound and put on the altar. Now God stopped Abraham at the crucial point and provided another sacrifice: it was a ram with its head caught in thorns. 'Behold the ram of God that takes away the sins of the world'. I don't like the word 'lamb' applied to Jesus. It is always portrayed as a little cuddly, white woolly thing in stained glass windows – it is a *ram*. No sacrifice was offered of a little cuddly lamb, it was a one-year old male ram with horns. And Jesus in the book of Revelation is the ram with seven horns – it is not a little cuddly picture, it is a strong picture, a *ram of God*. And God provided a ram for Abraham to offer in place of his son, a ram with his head caught in the thorns. God gave a new name to himself – I am always your Provider, Yahweh Jireh; God my Provider. And in that very mountain centuries later, another young man in his early thirties *was* sacrificed with his head caught in the thorns. Do you see there a picture of Jesus?

What about that strange encounter Abraham had with a man who was both a king and a priest, and who was king over the city Salem, which later became Jerusalem; and when Abraham was on his way back from a big battle to rescue his family who had been kidnapped, he came back with the spoils from the enemy and as he came near the city of Salem, which was then a pagan city, nothing to do with this godly line, but there was this strange figure Melchizedek, a priest *and* a king – that is a very unusual combination, never found in Israel. This king priest brought out *bread and wine* for Abraham and his troops, to refresh them and restore them, and Abraham gave him a tenth of all the spoils of the battle. And in our New Testament it says Jesus is a Priest forever after the order of Melchizedek: another little glimpse of our Lord Jesus Christ.

Let us go back to Jacob's ladder. Do you remember Jacob – the day he ran away from home, sleeping out at night with his head on a stone as a pillow, and he dreamt, and he saw not so much a ladder as an escalator? The Hebrew implies the ladder was moving, and there was one ladder moving up and one ladder moving down and there were angels ascending and descending and he felt that at the top of the ladders was heaven where God lived. He woke and that is when he promised to give a tenth of everything he made to God. Now, you see, a tithe was never part of the law until Moses. This was Jacob's *offer* of a tenth to bargain with God. If you bring me back home safely, I'll give you a tithe. But you can't bargain with God, you can't make a *contract* with God. God makes a *covenant* with you; he had to learn that the hard way later.

Centuries later, when Jesus said to Nathaniel: I saw you sitting under the fig tree, I noticed you – and you're a Jew in whom is no guile, no deceit; you're an honest Jew. And

Nathaniel said: how did you know that? He didn't deny it, but he acknowledged that Jesus knew him intimately. And Jesus said, you think that's wonderful? What will you think if you see angels ascending and descending on the Son of Man? An amazing thing to say, isn't it? He is saying: I'm Jacob's ladder, I'm the link between earth and heaven. I am the new ladder. Do you see Jesus in that instant? Jesus did.

Let us go way back to Genesis 3. God made a promise, even in the middle of his punishment. He said to the serpent that the seed – and the word is male – the seed of the woman will bruise your head even while you bruise his heel. Now bruising a heel is not fatal but bruising a head is, and that is the very first promise: that God would one day deal Satan a fatal blow. Who was this male seed of Eve who would do that? Well, you know who it was: it was the one who bound the strong man and spoiled his goods.

Let us go further back still to something I mentioned earlier. In Romans 5 Paul says: 'as one man's disobedience brought death, so one man's obedience brought life'. He is saying that Jesus is a second Adam, and both happened in a garden. It was in the Garden of Eden that Adam said, 'I won't' and it was in the Garden of Gethsemane that Jesus said, "Nevertheless not my will but yours be done." There is a contrast here. They both began a human race. Adam was the first man of *homo sapiens*. Jesus was the first human being of *homo novus*. I was born *homo sapiens*, I am now *homo novus*. The New Testament talks about the new man, the new humanity. In fact, there are two human races on earth today. You are born *homo sapiens*, you are born again *novus*. You are either in Adam or you are in Christ. There is a whole new human race and it is going to inhabit a totally new planet Earth, indeed a whole new universe.

Let us go even further. I suppose the most remarkable thing of all said about Jesus in the New Testament is that he was responsible for the creation of the universe. That a carpenter from Nazareth should ever be attributed with such an amazing achievement! But the early disciples came to see that Jesus was involved in Genesis chapter 1, and that, as they later said, 'without him nothing was made that has been made'. I once had the privilege of speaking at an open-air meeting in Canada in a place that had never seen a Christian meeting before, right in front of the Niagara Falls – now that's a backcloth! It was televised to the whole of Canada and parts of the USA. There were three speakers. I was put on first, then a Catholic priest then a Pentecostal pastor. We all talked about honeymoons. We hadn't prepared together, but actually Niagara is one of the honeymoon capitals of the world and all the hotels have bridal suites around the Falls. When I got up to speak, I said, "I'd like to tell you that I know the Man who made the Niagara Falls. I met him when I was 17 and we've been friends since." Well, they looked at me sideways as if I was crazy. I said: "His name actually is Jesus and without him nothing was made that has been made, so he made the Niagara Falls. Before he made chairs and tables he made the trees so he would have some timber, and before he preached the Sermon on the Mount, he made the mountains so he would have a pulpit."

Now this is remarkable really, isn't it, that a carpenter from Nazareth should be involved in creating our universe? So, when you read Genesis 1, do you see Jesus there? He is there – he is in the 'us': 'Let us make man in our own image'. We have known for many years that we are on an eggshell really, on flat plates of rock floating on molten rock and these plates are constantly moving, rubbing against each other, causing earthquakes. We are in a very delicate position really. We are just standing on these plates, and when this was discovered and the continental drift whereby the one piece of dry land that we read about in Genesis 1, drifted to become the continents of today, the scientists needed to coin a new word for these plates. And do you know what they called them? Tectonic plates, and do you know what the Greek word 'tectone' means, the word from which that adjective was coined? Tectone means 'carpenter'. Now I don't know if they were conscious of this when they chose that title. What a title! The whole planet earth on which we live was the result of a carpenter's work from Nazareth and his name is the Lord Jesus Christ.

We finish our studies where we began. We began with creation. We finish with Jesus Christ, *through whom* the world came to be and *for whom* it was made and *by whom* we discover the answer to our questions. For he is called in John chapter 1 the 'Logos' – the Word, but it means much more than the word. John wrote his Gospel in Ephesus and 500 years before John wrote that Gospel a man lived in Ephesus called Heraclites. He was the first real scientist, and he taught his students to observe and study what went on in animal life, in the weather, and he said everything you observe you must find out *the reason why* it behaves like it does. But the 'reason why' in Greek is logos and that has become the title of every branch of science – 'ology' means *the reason why*. Biology is the reason why life behaves as it does; zoology the reason why animals behave; psychology the reason why our minds behave as they do; sociology the reason why groups behave as they do; meteorology the reason why the weather behaves as it does. But every branch of science only looks at the reason why *part* of our universe behaves like it does. Nobody seems to be interested in the reason why it is *all* here and the answer is: Jesus is the reason why. He is *the* Logos of the whole universe. It was made for him and through him and by him, and to him be all praise and honour and glory and power for ever and ever. Amen.

APPENDIX

Visual aids used in the video sessions on Genesis *Unlocking the Bible* series arranged by parts

These graphical visual aids are intended for use as a supplement to the related recorded teaching sessions, providing illustrations which the author has used to accompany his talks. The sessions were delivered over a period of many decades, so some of the resources, where they refer to facts which were correct at the time of first use, may no longer be up-to-date. Some images will have been used in more than one talk, or in relation to more than one Bible study and provide, as far as possible, a full and appropriately accessible record of the resources used in each teaching series.

David Pawson's talks on
Unlocking the Bible can be found at:
www.davidpawson.org

or on the YouTube channel:
www.youtube.com/user/DavidPawsonMinistry

As indicated, they can also be used alongside and as a supplement to the book entitled *Unlocking the Bible* which can be purchased from the links below:

Buy the ebook: **www.davidpawson.com/utbbuykindle**
Buy the book: **www.davidpawson.com/utbbuybook**

GENESIS PART 1

GENESIS 1 – "GOD" 35x

GOD IS PERSONAL (heart, mind, will)
POWERFUL (10 commands obeyed)
UNCREATED (already, always there)
CREATIVE (imagination → variety)
ORDERLY (symmetry, mathematics)
SINGULAR (verbs)
PLURAL (noun)
GOOD (all he does because he is)
LOVING (wants to bless those he makes)
LIVING (active in this world)
SPEAKING (communicates to relate)
LIKE US (in his image)
UNLIKE US (we can't create)
NOT | IDENTIFIED WITH | HIS CREATION
    | DEPENDENT UPON |

GENESIS PART 2

HUMAN PHILOSOPHIES

ATHEISM: no God
AGNOSTICISM: don't know
ANIMISM: spirits are gods
POLYTHEISM: many gods
DUALISM: two gods < good / bad
MONOTHEISM: one God
DEISM: Creator can't control
THEISM: Creator can control

EXISTENTIALISM: experience is god
HUMANISM: man is god
RATIONALISM: reason is god
MATERIALISM: only matter is real
MYSTICISM: only spirit is real
MONISM: matter & spirit are one
PANTHEISM: all is god
PANENTHEISM: God is in all

BIBLICAL PHILOSOPHY

TRIUNETHEISM: 3 in 1 Creator controls creatures & creation

And God said,

Let:

$$\frac{1}{r^2}\frac{\partial}{\partial r}(r^2 D_r) + \frac{1}{r\sin\theta}\frac{\partial}{\partial \theta}(D_\theta \sin\theta) + \frac{1}{r\sin\theta}\frac{\partial D_\phi}{\partial \phi} = 4\pi\rho,$$

$$\frac{1}{r^2}\frac{\partial}{\partial r}(r^2 B_r) + \frac{1}{r\sin\theta}\frac{\partial}{\partial \theta}(B_\theta \sin\theta) + \frac{1}{r\sin\theta}\frac{\partial B_\phi}{\partial \phi} = 0;$$

$$\frac{1}{r\sin\theta}\left[\frac{\partial}{\partial \theta}(E_\phi \sin\theta) - \frac{\partial E_\theta}{\partial \phi}\right] = -\frac{1}{c}\frac{\partial B_r}{\partial t},$$

$$\frac{1}{r}\left[\frac{1}{\sin\theta}\frac{\partial E_r}{\partial \phi} - \frac{\partial}{\partial r}(rE_\phi)\right] = -\frac{1}{c}\frac{\partial B_\theta}{\partial t},$$

$$\frac{1}{r}\left[\frac{\partial}{\partial r}(rE_\theta) - \frac{\partial E_r}{\partial \theta}\right] = -\frac{1}{c}\frac{\partial B_\phi}{\partial t};$$

$$\frac{1}{r\sin\theta}\left[\frac{\partial}{\partial \theta}(H_\phi \sin\theta) - \frac{\partial H_\theta}{\partial \phi}\right] = 4\pi j_r + \frac{1}{c}\frac{\partial D_r}{\partial t},$$

$$\frac{1}{r}\left[\frac{1}{\sin\theta}\frac{\partial H_r}{\partial \phi} - \frac{\partial}{\partial r}(rH_\phi)\right] = 4\pi j_\theta + \frac{1}{c}\frac{\partial D_\theta}{\partial t},$$

$$\frac{1}{r}\left[\frac{\partial}{\partial r}(rH_\theta) - \frac{\partial H_r}{\partial \theta}\right] = 4\pi j_\phi + \frac{1}{c}\frac{\partial D_\phi}{\partial t};$$

and there was light.

GENESIS PART 2

STYLE: NOT SCIENTIFIC (HOW?)
BUT SIMPLISTIC (WHAT?)
  1. SUBJECT (GOD, WORD, SPIRIT)
  2. VERBS (CREATED, MADE)
  3. OBJECTS (DAYS 1-7)

STRUCTURE:

Uninhabitable	Uninhabited
GOD FORMS	GOD FILLS
Contrast	Content
1. LIGHT FROM DARKNESS	4. SUN AND MOON (+ stars)
2. SKY FROM OCEAN	5. BIRDS AND FISH
3. LAND FROM SEA (+plants)	6. ANIMALS AND HUMANS

7. DAY OFF!

LOGICAL: (simplified summary)
  1. BRICKLAYER
  2. CARPENTER
  3. PLUMBER
  4. ELECTRICIAN
  5. PLASTERER
  6. DECORATOR
  7. HOLIDAY

CHRONOLOGICAL: (critical path analysis)
  1. BRICKLAYER
  2. CARPENTER
  3. PLUMBER
  4. ELECTRICIAN
  5. PLASTERER
  6. DECORATOR
  7. HOLIDAYS

GENESIS PART 2

SCIENCE AND SCRIPTURE

1. **REPUDIATE**
   BELIEVERS DENY SCIENCE   UNBELIEVERS DENY SCRIPTURE

2. **SEGREGATE**
   SCIENCE — PHYSICAL TRUTH (WHEN? HOW?)
   SCRIPTURE — SPIRITUAL TRUTH (WHO? WHY?)
   WHERE IS LINE BETWEEN { MYTH AND HISTORY?
                          { VALUES AND FACTS ?

3. **INTEGRATE**
   TRANSITIONAL INVESTIGATIONS OF SCIENCE
   TRADITIONAL INTERPRETATIONS OF SCRIPTURE
   CREATION: SPEED (6 DAYS OR OVER 4 MILLION YEARS?)
   SEQUENCE (LIGHT BEFORE SUN, BIRDS BEFORE ANIMALS?)
   SELECTION (NATURAL OR SUPERNATURAL?)
   MAN: DERIVATION (MINERAL OR ANIMAL?)
   DURATION (DECADES OR CENTURIES?)
   DECEASE (NATURAL OR JUDICIAL?)
   FLOOD: EXTENT (LOCAL OR UNIVERSAL?)

"DAY" (Hebrew = YOM)

1. **LITERAL** (earth-day)
   a. Gap
   b. Flood
   c. Antique
2. **GEOLOGICAL** (age-day)
3. **MYTHOLOGICAL** (fable-day)
4. **EDUCATIONAL** (school-day)
   a. Verbal
   b. Visual
5. **THEOLOGICAL** (God-day)

   "all in a week's work"
   Note length of seventh day.

GENESIS PART 3

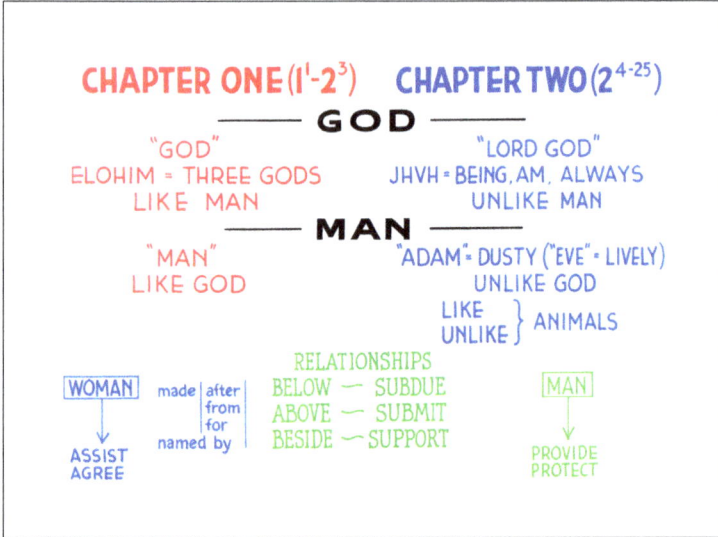

ORIGIN OF MAN

a. BIBLICAL   "let us.........our image"
                "created........from dust (woman from man)"

b. HISTORICAL Unity of human race
                  Agricultural archeology

c. PRE-HISTORIC   Homo sapiens
                    Neanderthal, Peking, Java, etc.
      SCIENCE — false investigation?
      SCRIPTURE — false information?

    a. PREHISTORIC WAS BIBLICAL (ie image of God)
        Gen 1: paleolithic hunter
        Gen 2: neolithic farmer (Adam not first man)

    b. PREHISTORIC BECAME BIBLICAL
        Did one, some, all change?
        'Sons of God and daughters of men'(Gen 6)

    c. PREHISTORIC NOT BIBLICAL
        Physical likeness, not spiritual
        Species now extinct

GENESIS PART 3

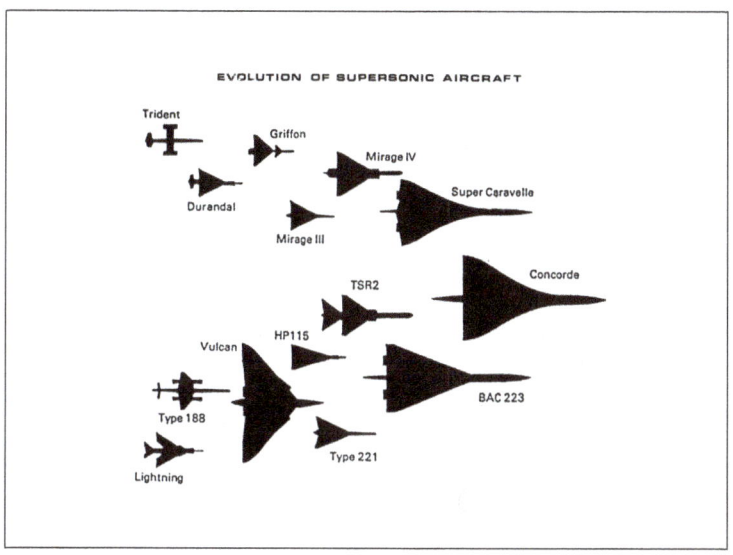

THEORY OF EVOLUTION
(TERMINOLOGY)

"VARIATION" ~ small, gradual changes in form
"SELECTION" ~ survival by suitability to environment
"NATURAL" ~ self-operating process (v. supernatural)
"MUTATION" ~ big, sudden changes in form (ie internal genes)

DARWIN   LAMARCH

MICRO-EVOLUTION
    Limited development within different groups
MACRO-EVOLUTION
    Total development from single origin

"STRUGGLE" ~ survival of the fittest
(key-word)

GENESIS PART 3

1. MENTAL CHOICE

CREATION	EVOLUTION
Father God	Mother nature
Personal choice	Impersonal chance
Designed purpose	Random pattern
Supernatural production	Natural process
Open situation	Closed system
Providence	Coincidence
Faith based on fact	Faith based on fancy
God free to make man in his image	Man free to make God in his image / imagination

2. MORAL CHOICE

CREATION	EVOLUTION
God is Lord	Man is lord
Divine authority	Human autonomy
Absolute standards	Relative situations
Duty - responsibility	Demand- rights
'Infant' dependence	'Adult' independence
Man fallen	Man rising
Salvation of weak	Survival of strong
Right is might	Might is right
Peace	War
Obedience	Indulgence
Faith, hope and love	Fatalism, helplessness and luck
Heaven	Hell

GENESIS PART 4

FLOOD SEDIMENT IN MESOPOTAMIA

ANIMALS ENTER ARK

GENESIS PART 4

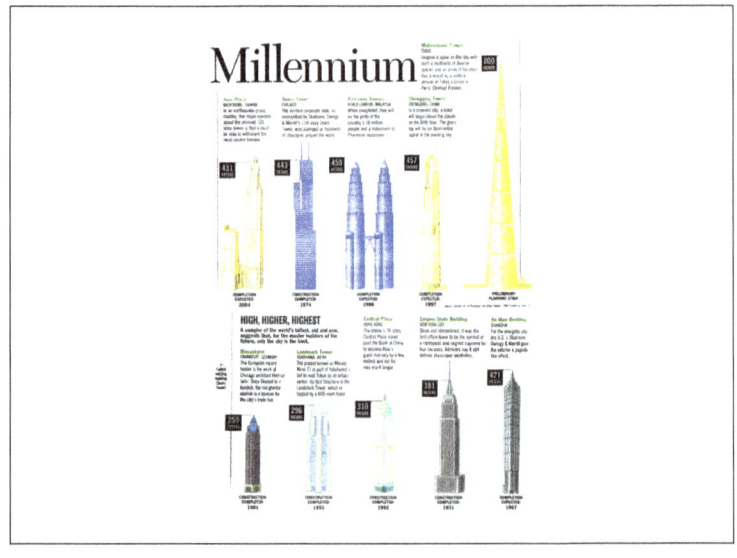

GENESIS PART 4

GENESIS 1-11 & CHINESE WRITING

CREATE: 造

DEVIL: 鬼

TEMPTER: 魔

BOAT: 船

土 = mud
丿 = life, motion
辶 = walking
儿 = man, son
田 = garden
厶 = secret, private
'devil' + 木木 = two trees
广 = cover
丼 = container
八 = eight
口 = mouth, person

GENESIS PART 5

OUTLINE OF GENESIS

1-11
Short section (¼)
Long Period (centuries)
Many people (nations)

12-50
Long section (¾)
Short period (years)
Few people (family)

1-2 GOOD CREATOR
DIVINE ACTIONS
HUMAN RELATIONS

12-36 GOD OF ABRAHAM v. LOT
ISAAC v. ISHMAEL
JACOB v. ESAU

3-11 BAD CREATURES
FALL
FALL OUT

37-50 JOSEPH OF GOD
DOWN TO PRISONER
UP TO PREMIER

ZIGGURAT IN UR

GENESIS PART 5

FIREPLACE IN UR

JORDAN VALLEY

GENESIS PART 5

LOT'S WIFE

PETRA

ABOUT DAVID PAWSON

A speaker and author with uncompromising faithfulness to the Holy Scriptures, David brings clarity and a message of urgency to Christians to uncover hidden treasures in God's Word.

Born in England in 1930, David began his career with a degree in Agriculture from Durham University. When God intervened and called him to become a Minister, he completed an MA in Theology at Cambridge University and served as a Chaplain in the Royal Air Force for three years. He moved on to pastor several churches, including the Millmead Centre in Guildford, which became a model for many UK church leaders. In 1979, the Lord led him into an international ministry. His current itinerant ministry is predominantly to church leaders. David and his wife Enid currently reside in the county of Hampshire in the UK.

Over the years, he has written a large number of books, booklets, and daily reading notes. His extensive and very accessible overviews of the books of the Bible have been published and recorded in *Unlocking the Bible*. Millions of copies of his teachings have been distributed in more than 120 countries, providing a solid biblical foundation.

He is reputed to be the "most influential Western preacher in China" through the broadcast of his best-selling *Unlocking the Bible* series into every Chinese province by Good TV. In the UK, David's teachings are often broadcast on Revelation TV.

Countless believers worldwide have also benefited from his generous decision in 2011 to make available his extensive audio video teaching library free of charge at **www.davidpawson.org** and we have recently uploaded all of David's video to a dedicated channel on **www.youtube.com**

TAKE A LOOK AT YOUTUBE
www.youtube.com/user/DavidPawsonMinistry

THE EXPLAINING SERIES
BIBLICAL TRUTH SIMPLY EXPLAINED

If you have been blessed reading this book, we have more books available in David's Explaining Series. Please register to download for free by visiting
www.explainingbiblicaltruth.global

Other booklets in the *Explaining* series include:
The Amazing Story of Jesus
The Resurrection: *The Heart of Christianity*
Studying the Bible
Being Anointed and Filled with the Holy Spirit
New Testament Baptism
How to study a book of the Bible: Jude
The Key Steps to Becoming a Christian
What the Bible says about Money
What the Bible says about Work
Grace – *Undeserved Favour, Irresistible Force or Unconditional Forgiveness?*
Eternally secure? – *What the Bible says about being saved*
De-Greecing the Church – The impact of Greek thinking on Christian beliefs
Three texts often taken out of context: *Expounding the truth and exposing error*
The Trinity
The Truth about Christmas

They will also be available to purchase as print copies from:
Amazon or **www.thebookdepository.com**

ALSO AVAILABLE

A COMMENTARY ON GENESIS
CHAPTERS 1–25

ISBN 978-1-911173-82-3

Readers of Introducing Genesis who wish to go deeper will appreciate this latest addition to Anchor's growing range of Bible Commentaries.

This Commentary explains in depth the immense significance of the first twenty-five chapters of Genesis. We are shown how the great themes of these opening chapters of scripture are relevant in every age and indeed are essential to the whole of God's self-revelation throughout the Bible.

As always, David Pawson's lively, accessible teaching style makes this an engaging read with enduring appeal.

OTHER TEACHINGS
BY DAVID PAWSON

For the most up to date list of David's Books
go to: **www.davidpawsonbooks.com**

To purchase David's Teachings
go to: **www.davidpawson.com**

UNLOCKING THE BIBLE

A unique overview of both the Old and New Testaments, from internationally acclaimed evangelical speaker and author David Pawson. *Unlocking the Bible* opens up the Word of God in a fresh and powerful way. Avoiding the small detail of verse by verse studies, it sets out the epic story of God and his people in Israel. The culture, historical background and people are introduced and the teaching applied to the modern world. Eight volumes have been brought into one compact and easy to use guide to cover both the Old and New Testaments in one massive omnibus edition. *The Old Testament: The Maker's Instructions* (The five books of law); *A Land and A Kingdom* (Joshua, Judges, Ruth, 1&2 Samuel, 1&2 Kings); *Poems of Worship and Wisdom* (Psalms, Song of Solomon, Proverbs, Ecclesiastes, Job); *Decline and Fall of an Empire* (Isaiah, Jeremiah and other prophets); *The Struggle to Survive* (Chronicles and prophets of exile); *The New Testament: The Hinge of History* (Mathew, Mark, Luke, John and Acts); *The Thirteenth Apostle* (Paul and his letters); *Through Suffering to Glory* (Hebrews, the letters of James, Peter and Jude, the Book of Revelation). Already an international bestseller.

WATCH DAVID'S INTRO
www.davidpawson.com/utbintro

WATCH
www.davidpawson.com/utbwatch

LISTEN
www.davidpawson.com/utblisten

PURCHASE THE BOOK
www.davidpawson.com/utbbuybook

PURCHASE THE EBOOK
www.davidpawson.com/utbbuykindle

PURCHASE THE DVD
www.davidpawson.com/utbbuydvd

PURCHASE USB • ALL VIDEO (MP4)
FLASH DRIVE INCLUDING: • ALL AUDIO TRACKS (MP3)
• CHARTS (PDF)
www.davidpawson.com/buyusb

OTHER LANGUAGES

Unlocking the Bible is available in book, video and audio formats and has been translated into other languages.

www.ingramcontent.com/pod-product-compliance
Lightning Source LLC
Chambersburg PA
CBHW070955080526
44587CB00015B/2312